T0367779

AMERICAN URBAN FORM

Urban and Industrial Environments
Series editor: Robert Gottlieb, Henry R. Luce Professor of Urban and
Environmental Policy, Occidental College

For a complete list of books published in this series, please see the back of the book.

American Urban Form

A Representative History

Sam Bass Warner and Andrew H. Whittemore

drawings by Andrew H. Whittemore

The MIT Press   Cambridge, Massachusetts   London, England

First MIT Press paperback edition, 2013

This book was set in Adobe Garamond by the MIT Press.

Library of Congress Cataloging-in-Publication Data
Warner, Sam Bass, 1928–
  American urban form : a representative history / Sam Bass Warner and Andrew H. Whittemore ; drawings by Andrew H. Whittemore.
    p. cm. — (Urban and industrial environments)
Includes bibliographical references and index.
ISBN 978-0-262-01721-3 (hardcover : alk. paper)—978-0-262-52532-9 (pb. : alk. paper)
1. Cities and towns—United States—History. 2. City and town life—United States—History.
I. Whittemore, Andrew H., 1980–II. Title
HT123.W228 2012
307.760973—dc23
2011033010

For Diana, Carole, and John

Contents

Acknowledgments   ix

Introduction   1

1   The City's Seventeenth-Century Beginnings   8

2   The City in the Mid-Eighteenth Century   20

3   The Merchant Republic, 1820   32

4   The City Overwhelmed, 1860   48

5   The City Restructured, 1895   64

6   Toward a New Economy and a Novel Urban Form, 1925   84

7   The Federally Supported City, 1950   102

8   The Polycentric City, 1975   118

9   The Global City, 2000   136

Notes   155

Suggested Reading   161

Index   173

Series List   181

ACKNOWLEDGMENTS

In the years since we began working on this project, many people have helped and encouraged us. The Young Research Library at the University of California Los Angeles proved a valuable resource, as did the Rotch Library at the Massachusetts Institute of Technology and its skilled librarians Peter Cohn and Ann Whiteside. Professors Eugenie Ladner Birch at the University of Pennsylvania, Lawrence Vale and Eran Ben-Joseph at MIT, and Anastasia Loukaitou-Sideris at UCLA have given readings, support, and encouragement. Albert La Farge, our agent, has made important suggestions for improvement, as did Diana J. Kleiner who has read several versions with great care and perspicacity. We would also like to thank Clay Morgan at the MIT Press.

Sam Bass Warner
Andrew H. Whittemore

Introduction

This book is about patterns, the physical patterns or "urban form" that we can observe in American big cities past and present. It is also about the social, political, economic, and other human patterns that these physical patterns shape and are themselves shaped by in turn.

The term "urban form" refers to the spaces, places, and boundaries that define urban life. Urban forms are composed of houses, buildings, streets, parks, market farms, pipes and wires, railroads, highways, wharves, and airports. Any particular urban form reflects the complex interrelationships among social, economic, and political processes that brought it into being. New resources, new technologies, new ways of doing business, the migration of peoples, and shifts in politics and culture all have their part to play in the building and altering of urban form. Planning for a city's future requires that such forces be discussed and evaluated, because they are the tools of urban change.

We have written this book for two groups of people: citizens who are now concerned about the conditions of American urban living, and their allies—city planners, architects, landscape architects, civil engineers, and municipal officials—the professionals with whom they must work to preserve or alter these patterns to improve the places in which they live. We write at a time when the great majority of Americans live in metropolitan areas, when a new world economy and global environmental crises are forcing cities—both urban form and ways of living within it—to change.

It is our belief that the most effective way to open a discussion of choices among future alternatives is to review where we have been. To this end, this book imagines a hypothetical city, which we simply refer to as "the City," to identify patterns and trends common to the history of many American cities over the past three hundred years. Rather than examine the particulars of a single city, we have instead reviewed the histories of three major cities—Boston, Philadelphia, and New York—to identify the spatial arrangements, public events, and social practices common to all three that make up key patterns in past American urban development. "The City" is therefore neither New York nor Boston nor Philadelphia but a composite of the experience of each. Where the narrative gives a specific date, we include it because we are referring to telling events from the past that illustrate the conditions of that era. Quantities are also given to help the reader judge the scale of the City and its elements—distances, heights of buildings, and population. These estimates are approximations that suggest the common experience of the three cities out of which the hypothetical was fashioned.

This book is composed of two complementary elements. First, the changing physical patterns of urban form are captured in original pen-and-ink drawings (done without the aid of any graphics software) that describe the City visually. Second, this visual account is accompanied by a text that describes the history of the forces that built and rebuilt the urban form of the City and some of the ways of urban living that arose within it. The text does so by synthesizing events from the three cities that make up the composite City. Thus, wages and work produced a specific distribution of people within the City, but the culture of the residents and their politics influenced what was built.

One might argue that the situation of our three cities—located as they are on the Atlantic seaboard, at one end of the continent—made them unique. All American cities, however, began at the end of something: a trail, a landing along a river or lake, a railroad. Although each city has a unique history and character, therefore, it also shares physical, economic, and social trends and experience common to all American cities.

The hypothetical City pictured and described in this book demonstrates the common underlying urban form established first in older cities as they changed from European village beachhead to merchant seaport, industrial city, multicentered metropolis, and finally regional metropolis. More recently in American history, the tendencies experienced by our three older cities have been repeated in metropolises such as Chicago, Los Angeles, and the Sunbelt cities of the South and Southwest. Our identification of key shared patterns that have composed urban form we offer as a helpful resource to the citizens and professionals of any large American city.

Actual examples from the past, rather than generalizations from such examples, best capture the varieties of response that residents brought to the forms they inherited and built. The illustrations, events, and descriptions of adaptations selected for inclusion here clearly reveal interactions between urban residents and the physical forms within which they lived. Although they explain commonalities in the evolution of the three cities of Boston, Philadelphia, and New York, however, our intention is not to make a *comparative* urban history but rather to create a single rich and detailed picture of urban form and its impact.

This book invites readers to acquaint themselves with the urban form around them in several ways. Studying a city is first of all a visual sport. Professional urbanists start their research by walking around and driving about. During the 1960s this way of learning brought forth a number of important books that redirected planning practices. The city planner Kevin Lynch began his studies by walking blocks in Boston to learn what information the streets and buildings offered pedestrians. Later he mounted a camera behind the windshield of a car and drove along highways to study the experiences of highway travel. In New York City at the same time a magazine writer who rode about town on her bicycle, Jane Jacobs, used her observations to challenge both city and suburban planning. Her Hudson Street daily ballet, a report on the passage of people along her block, is an exercise every urban and suburban resident should repeat as a way to learn their environment. Gordon Cullen, an architect, walked about London observing sequences of new and old buildings, and then wrote a descriptive critique of what he saw. His book stimulated a new approach to urban design by stressing the importance of attending to the merits of existing buildings as they shape a street or block. During the 1970s Jan Gehl walked about Copenhagen with his camera, recording the outdoor spaces and activities of that city. He focused his attention on the small outdoor spaces that make it a pleasant place to live, and he worked successfully to change city policies to make more such spaces.

To observe a current city, surely walking about its neighborhoods and driving through its surrounding metropolitan region are good ways to form mental pictures of how the groupings of buildings shape the social and economic activities they afford. In fact, so many families have jobs and errands that require cross commuting within their urban region that they come to have ideas for making travel easier. Since driving is such a universal experience, here is a promising topic to begin any discussion of potential changes for a city.

To experience the urban form of earlier times requires a little thought and imagination. If you measure out a mile and walk that distance, you will know the common commuting distance of residents before the advent of electric streetcars. Few cities have preserved or refashioned their streetcar lines, but chances are that many popular bus routes repeat old streetcar routes. Furthermore, where major rail lines still exist, a motorist can discover along them some of the original industrial and commercial corridors of a city.

Such exploration will lead citizens toward the concerns of two scholarly groups, the land economists and the sociologists. The economists chart and try to predict changes in land values in a metropolitan region. Why are rents high here and low there? What accounts for large tracts of land of modest price? Unless a citizen consults the official records of the Assessor's Office, the data of the economists and their mathematical models will be out of reach. But, by thinking about the location of buildings and activities, a citizen can estimate the value relationships, if not the exact rents or land prices, of areas of the city. Density of buildings and activity are a reliable indicator of high land prices and rents. They also reflect the consequences of zoning laws that have been put in place in our cities and suburbs since the 1920s.

If one understands that the transportation patterns and ways of doing business in a city have been altered over time, as indeed they have often been in the past, then the previous geographies of a city emerge. With such insights the citizen is in a position to consider what aspects of urban life he or she would like to maintain and what others to change.

Sociologists of the city followed quickly upon the first economic commentary. The pricing of land, they realized, played a major role in determining who lived where. Because the wealthy could afford the most desirable locations away from smoke and toil, here well-to-do families appeared. Every American city has its axis of fashionable apartment houses and comfortable suburbs. A few sociologists followed the fashionable, but most concerned themselves with the circumstances of immigrants and the poor. The issue is still before us, and a citizen might well ask, "Where are the immigrants and poor living in my city and region?" A next question might well be, "Is my neighborhood open to all comers, or does some combination of rents and social exclusion keep the poor and the disfavored away?" Such questions that start with house prices and rents soon demand an assessment of the cultures and politics of the city and its neighborhoods.

Thus, the significance of urban form for the citizen amateur overlaps its significance for the professional planner and urban scholar. All need to understand and consider the core values that animate city building. The values of capitalism and democracy have long stood at the base of our culture, and their conflicts and agreements have shaped our past. These same values undergird our hopes for the future. Yet within such a general cultural frame, for all its seeming permanence the urban form of all cities is ever-changing and thereby offers each generation a fresh chance to refresh and reform, improve and advance the world around us.

I

THE CITY'S SEVENTEENTH-CENTURY BEGINNINGS

Figure 1.1 The City as it appeared in the late seventeenth century.

The First People of the City

The geological structures of rivers and the ocean gave enduring shape to the City. Here, where a deep estuary entered into a sheltered bay off the Atlantic Ocean, Europeans would make their first forays into the region. This estuary would one day serve as the city's harbor. Along the edge of the bay the land formed dramatic headlands that would prove good sites for fortifications by European settlers. About two miles inland from the bay, a small river originating in inland freshwater lakes entered the estuary. The river flowed into the estuary from the north, but wound shortly before its end so as to form a small peninsula that would serve as the site of the first permanent settlement and the birthplace of the European city. The marshes and shallow coves of the estuary were rich in shellfish, while the inland was heavily wooded and dotted with freshwater lakes left from the glaciers that had receded 10,000 years before. The glaciers also left behind shallow and rocky topsoil that sat above granite bedrock, up from which bubbled numerous springs. Winters were long and cold, and summers brief though very hot and humid. These basic elements established the environments within which the communities of Amerindians lived, and later they set the frame for the Europeans.

The tribes of the Atlantic region from Massachusetts to Pennsylvania did not live in permanent settlements fortified by wooden palisades until they learned such ways from the Europeans. Instead of a permanent village, they moved back and forth over a small territory of hunting and fishing grounds as the seasons compelled. In the late fall, they and their packs of hunting dogs moved into the forest to hunt the fattened deer and bears. In early spring, the tribes built weirs and fished in the herring, shad, and salmon runs. Then came planting time and a summer of gathering berries and harvesting. They fashioned their tools, weapons, and ornaments from stone, wood, bone, and shells, and by firing clay they made pots, clay pipes, and effigies of birds, animals, and people.

Temporary residence determined the forms of their settlements. The tribal members gathered together according to matrilineal descent. For shelter they placed conical teepees of bark and grass and domed round houses near fire pits, and raised rectangular longhouses of bark where they settled for some months. The Atlantic tribes lacked the chiefs found among the Five Nations to the West and also had no intertribal organization. Archaeological remains suggest that little trade moved from tribe to tribe until the arrival of many Europeans.

The sixteenth century inaugurated continuing relations between these long-settled peoples and European fishermen and explorers. The visitors offered iron tools, copper pots, woven cloth, and alcohol, while the Indians reciprocated with hospitality, corn, game, beaver and otter furs, and by teaching the use of tobacco. A century of epidemics—smallpox, typhus, measles, and diphtheria—followed, decimating the native population so that when Europeans opened their first permanent settlements on the coast in the early seventeenth century they faced few Indian neighbors.

An easy peace never followed the beginnings of settlement. Neighboring tribes continued to supply furs until the beaver and otter had been trapped out. For a time in the 1620s and 1630s, the coastal tribes' manufacture of shell beads and wampum gave them a significant role in the European beaver trade to the north and west. Yet, with newcomers ceaselessly advancing over their hunting grounds, no satisfactory mutual peace could be fashioned. Fraud, theft, and violence on both sides led to sporadic warfare and even bitter wars of extinction like King Philip's War, 1675–1676. The eastern tribes tried to forestall their loss of land by repeated sales of the same small parcels, but in time they had to surrender their ground. Europeans drove them into small reservations surrounded by European settlers. Others fled to caves, swamps, and the rough lands near their former territory. Some sought places among the northern and western tribes, whose conflicts with the European frontier became enmeshed in the imperial battles between France and England. By 1700 the City had but a few tribal descendants, mainly Indians working as servants and laborers living among the Europeans.

Fragments of peace stand out in this bitter record. Reverend John Eliot of Roxbury, Massachusetts, converted and established a town for his "Praying Indians," but he was unable to adequately protect them. The Indians that settled among the Moravians in Pennsylvania seem to have fared better. Most remarkable of all the bargains and promises was William Penn's one success. He promised the tribes of nearby New Jersey that if they had complaints about the behavior of European settlers, he would call a conference of representatives of both sides to adjudicate the issues. The procedure was initiated once, but never again. Even Penn could not imagine Amerindians as citizens.

So began 250 years of continental conquest and a seemingly ceaseless cultural conflict. War and cultural conflict were, in fact, the hallmarks of seventeenth-century Europe. Racked by imperial rivalries and terrible religious wars between

Protestants and Catholics, the Europeans added to the century's horrors by their participation in the African slave trade and the establishment of African slavery in the New World.

The Founding of a Colony

In such a violent climate, armed merchant trading corporations endeavored to tap the riches of both the Orient and the Americas. New York's beginnings give an apt example of the typical conflicts and achievements of the first years of Atlantic settlements. The first shiploads of settlers, African slaves, and domestic animals landed in 1626 to begin the City. Planting, trading, and shelter, everything had to get under way all at once. Meadows and wild grasses made a pasture for the cattle, but 20 were lost from their eating unfamiliar poisonous plants. The farmers in the group planted former Amerindian fields in mid-May to harvest grain in August. The settlers managed about "30 mean hovels made of the bark of trees" while others sought shelter in holes. They fed on fish and oysters, but their familiar milk and butter remained in short supply for several years.[1]

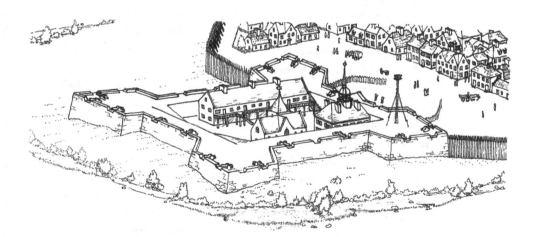

Figure 1.2 Where the river entered the harbor the settlers had constructed a stone fortress by the close of the seventeenth century, replacing an earlier wooden structure. The fortress was constructed on the European model, with bastions for artillery. It also housed a barracks and a church. Where it faced the City there was a wide parade ground.

Fearing "the savages . . . and enemies from abroad," the pioneers began an earthen fort next the harbor at one corner of their beachhead. They lacked the manpower, however, to fashion proper stone-faced walls, so that a few years later the walls had been trodden down by cattle and rooted up by pigs.[2] Only after several decades did the settlers manage to construct any permanent fortress. They also built a smaller second fort at the entrance to the harbor on the headlands.

Trade took a preeminent place, with the consequence that business and the fort together set the frame for the City's first and oldest remaining street system. For the corporation the settlers managed to erect a small stone countinghouse, its roof thatched with reeds. They placed it near the beach landing of the harbor. Here the company's agent gathered and taxed the exports of furs trapped by the Amerindians. A horse-powered mill also had been constructed so that the first return shipment included some sawed timber with the furs.

All the land within miles of the settlement belonged to the corporation from its royal grant. The agent paced out and staked house lots and assigned farm acreages, but he lacked a formal plan like that of Philadelphia. The settlers, after drawing lots for their parcels, were obliged to construct a house on their assigned property and to pay a small rent. In time the corporation transferred these leaseholds to private property ownership.[3]

Out of this process the elements of the forms of a European village emerged. Next to the fort on the town side a wide parade ground was set aside. In time this space became the site of public markets and the street grew in length, becoming a "Broad Way" leading from the fort to the farms beyond. In later years the corporation was able to fit out the fort with stone facings and a barracks for soldiers. The village also erected a fifteen-foot wooden palisade to enclose and defend the twenty small blocks of the settlement, later replaced by a stone-faced wall featuring small batteries.

In the early years the shore landing, the Strand, proved the more powerful organizing principle of the town's form. An enlarged corporate countinghouse and storehouse stood here at one arm of a wharf. From this commercial center narrow streets ran into the interior at right angles to the waterline. Families, servants, and slaves crowded into small two-and-a-half-story timber houses lining the streets. Narrow but deep, the tiny blocks afforded back gardens and a few fruit trees in their interiors. By 1680 a few of the outer blocks near the wall boasted houses of the wealthy merchants. Given larger lots, they enjoyed spacious gardens, even a few laid out in the formal geometry that seventeenth-century

Figure 1.3 Outside of the City, settlers built a small settlement arranged around a common, which supplied common grazing land for the inhabitants' animals. The common was also the site of a meeting house and cemetery.

fashion decreed. None of these houses of the first decades survive to the present, but the street pattern still orders the oldest blocks of today's City. A tavern, brew houses, a jail, a poorhouse, a large church, and a governor's mansion completed the town's facilities. The corporation housed its African slaves outside the wall.

In time the rural fringe served the City by provisioning its stalls in the weekly markets. Even in these first decades, resident wealthy merchants and influential stockholders in the chartered company set out large gentlemen's farms on lands that would later be absorbed by the City. One satellite village of the City, established by Puritans, took the New England form of a common with a meetinghouse and small house plots clustered about, its religious orientation a departure from the business and military dominance of the city itself.

Unpaved streets made for a dusty town in summer and muddy ruts and puddles in winter. Pigs and goats rooted in the garbage thrown from the houses, stinking privies overflowed, and the thatched roofs and clay-lined wooden chimneys of the first years fed numerous fires. After a few decades, the town fathers endeavored to make a safer and more orderly town. They purchased leather buckets to be placed on every street corner to serve in case of fire. Wooden chimneys and thatched roofs were forbidden and brick construction encouraged. Ordinances required fences in an attempt to control the damage of the wandering pigs and goats, and in 1675 weekly trash collection began. No hospitals existed, but a European-trained doctor and midwives visited the sick, injured, and pregnant. As in London, women took the sick into their own homes to nurse.

The Political Scene

The turmoil of seventeenth-century Europe fostered the cultural diversity of the City's early settlers. Merchants from Amsterdam, London, Le Havre, Lisbon, and Cadiz traded across the world from Japan to Peru. As they sailed, they left behind a world sundered by rapid change: behind them in their home countries the established orders of the European village and town were torn apart by new wealth, imperial ambitions, and religious conflict. These three orientations shaped the City from its first beginnings.

Although the seventeenth century is honored today for the beginnings of the Enlightenment and the scientific revolution, most contemporaries held up religion as the lens through which they sought to glimpse the possibilities of their tumultuous world. Puritans from England came to the North American shores of New England in hopes of finding a rich land where they might establish orderly communities of young people. Their new city might be likened to a school. The literate citizens would read and be taught by a learned minister. Indeed, this need for an educated ministry gave rise to North America's first college at Cambridge, Massachusetts, in 1636. By such means, the Puritans expected to establish a more enlightened order than what the confining traditions of the English village afforded.

In these same years the Quakers settled on the Delaware. A group of English Protestants, they wished to establish a peaceful and charitable community among themselves without resort to militia and wars. Both Puritan and Quaker settlements and the overtaken Dutch colonies of New York owed their existence to the worldwide trade of Europe, especially the trade between the West Indies, the Spanish Empire, and Brazil. Because of this far-reaching trade, people of every religious belief crowded in among the sectarians. As the English colonial governor of New York observed in 1687, his town contained Calvinists,

Lutherans, a few Catholics, orthodox Quakers, "Singing Quakers, Ranting Quakers, Sabbatarians, Anti-Sabbatarians, some Anabaptists, some Independents, some Jews; in short, of all sorts of opinions there are some, and the most part of none at all."[4]

Although the City represented a new chance in a new land for the similar mixture of peoples who settled there, and all early settlers obtained a plot of land of their own, former position in the old country plus wealth and family connections established a class hierarchy here. After a few decades, the merchants, fur traders, ship captains, shipbuilders, and distillers made up the top quarter of the City's population and owned two-thirds of its wealth.

Beneath them stood the class Benjamin Franklin would later call the "leather apron men," craftsmen whose skill was their wealth. These artisans—masons, blacksmiths, coopers, house and ship carpenters, sail makers, shoemakers, hatters, tailors, wheelwrights, millers, bakers, and schoolmasters—sustained the new City. Making up the second-highest quarter of its population, they owned a quarter of its wealth. Beneath them lived an itinerant population of laborers and sailors, mostly young people with hopes but small fortunes. Because in the first decades of settlement labor was in such high demand, the town did not suffer a poverty problem in the later sense of an unemployed and indigent class. Long and severe winters, storms, sickness, and wars, however, brought suffering the able bodied laborers and their families close to starvation. The few disabled, orphaned, or widowed found care in municipal charity.

Most households harbored an apprentice and a young man or woman who was an indentured servant. Very often, too, they kept an African slave. Settlers had purchased slaves from the very outset of their settlement, and during the seventeenth century perhaps one in five households owned a slave. The ratio grew to two in five households by the end of the century.[5] A few slaves managed to purchase their freedom, and there had been an experiment with "half freedom" whereby slaves were allowed to farm on their own if they paid an annual tax, but their children remained the property of their owner. In these harsh times, many slaves died from overwork, and there is evidence of despairing mothers killing their infants.

As an English colony, the City patterned its institutions and society on the old country, thereby suffering many of the latter's limitations and conflicts. A governor appointed usually by the Crown ruled with a provincial assembly of the wealthy. Together they established the laws and appointed the judges. By and large, they endeavored to keep order according to the brutal customs of the day, including public whippings and public executions. They also used their position to establish trading monopolies and to acquire prime parcels of land. In times of war, the governor issued letters of marque authorizing syndicates to outfit ships to capture the merchantmen of enemy countries, France or Spain. In some years during these imperial wars, the demarcation between legitimate privateer and criminal pirate became so blurred that the City earned a reputation as a nest of pirates.

The royal governor also granted the City a charter so it might govern itself. The charter repeated a similar pattern of privilege, but a role was reserved for owners of taxable property. They might elect the town's constable, tax assessor, aldermen, mayor, and councilors. Such institutions sufficed to hire a nightly watchman, offer a little charity, regulate the markets and set the price of a loaf of bread, organize a militia company, and maintain a rough and ready order against tavern brawls and petty thievery.

The City's crude governance broke down, however, when religious conflict spilled over from Europe. Although it was but an overgrown village on the Atlantic shore far from the European centers of empire, the traffic of the ocean made it vulnerable to distant conflicts. Warfare always disrupts the order of any society, and the City, a new town of strangers, proved especially vulnerable.

In 1685, Louis XIV revoked the edict of toleration for French Protestants (Huguenots), thereby sending thousands fleeing to Holland, England, and overseas. A good number settled in the City, becoming rivals of the established English elite. Next, in 1688, James II, an English Catholic king, fled his country when confronted by a popular uprising and a mob supported by a small Dutch army. This "Glorious Revolution" made William of Orange king of England, but it destroyed the royal authority in several Atlantic colonies where an unpopular English governor had been trying to enlarge his powers. A mob in one colony dragged the governor off to jail and sent him in chains on a ship bound for England.[6]

In the City, the royal governor grew helpless while unity among the citizens frayed. Strong passions divided the town between supporters of established privileges and supporters of ordinary citizens. Amid cries against the "grandees," new men were voted in. A Huguenot, an immigrant merchant who had been a militia leader, was elected mayor and later declared commander-in-chief of the province. He abolished the colony's monopolies. When in 1691 war broke out between England and the scourge of Protestants, Louis XIV of France (King William's War, or the War of the League of Augsburg, 1691–1697), the commander made a failed attempt to attack Canada.

Finally, at the end of March 1691, King William's troops arrived with a new patent for a royal governor. The acting governor and his partner, as a reward for all their services, were hanged as traitors to the Crown. Theirs was the City's first rebellion against royal authority. It set no legal precedent, but it revealed the weakness of imperial governance and the tensions in the social fabric within the City. The rebellion's themes of conflict and class advantage would echo through the City in ensuing years.[7]

2

THE CITY IN THE MID-EIGHTEENTH CENTURY

Figure 2.1 The City as it appeared in the mid-eighteenth century.

The City and the World

By the mid-eighteenth century, despite wars and epidemics of smallpox, measles, typhus, typhoid, and the annual fall scourge of malaria, the City had grown to be a substantial colonial outpost of about 18,000 inhabitants. Its progress exceeded French Quebec's 8,500, but powerful Amerindian tribes closed off its western reach so that it lagged far behind Spanish America. There Havana boasted 35,000 residents and Mexico City had grown to 100,000. Lacking a populous farming interior, the City had been unable to grow as fast as its contemporary British trading post, Calcutta (founded 1686), now a city of 115,000.

The form of the city reflected its global role. Fortifications were strengthened; on occasions when wars threatened, soldiers and the navy dominated. The forts and their garrisons were to defend the city in the event of foreign wars and also to be available to quell riots of angry citizens. When the troops departed for imperial adventures in the Caribbean or against French Canada, city dwellers feared for their safety.

The City's economy had shifted away from its seventeenth-century base of furs and fish. Now timber and sawed lumber, iron, and farm crops of oats, wheat, barley, and flour dominated the export trade. Oceangoing ships even served as exports. Vessels constructed in the City's yards were outfitted for a voyage to London where both the ship and its cargo were sold. The exports in turn financed the importation of English and European products. Complex exchanges followed trade routes to the West Indies, Africa, the Mediterranean, France, England, and Holland.

In such an Atlantic trading economy, those merchant families with connections to Court and to major London merchants held a big advantage. The bolder among them chanced illegal trading with the West Indies and even supported pirate attacks in the West Indies, Red Sea, and Indian Ocean. By midcentury the City began to show evidence of this merchant wealth: the royal governor's house, a few fine mansions, some carriages, and some country seats.

The City Takes Shape

Farms and farm villages composed the immediate surroundings of the City. These, and others located along the rivers to the interior, fed the City and supplied it with its major export commodities. The City itself was composed of hundreds of small multipurpose dwellings: brick ones for the prosperous, wood for the poor and for fresh bachelor immigrants.

Underneath the entire settlement—the City and its neighboring farms—lay a sort of economic time bomb, the future promise of a monopoly of urban space in the midst of an abundance of open land. The settling corporation had given out large tracts or smaller but locationally favorable parcels to early settlers according to their social rank and also according to their investment in the company's shares. Others received farms or favored smaller plots if they were friends of the governor or if they were important merchants whose favor the governor sought. Still another few were members of the closed municipal corporation, in a position for special opportunities. Out of such a pattern of land distribution the City's steep class hierarchy emerged. Yet, despite these privileges, it took fifty years of further city growth to raise land prices sufficiently to make the advantaged families rich from renting real estate. At midcentury, houses and land next the central docks and stores had become expensive, and some of the poor had been driven to the outer edges of town where the cheapest wooden buildings could be found. Despite these small changes, mixed blocks and alleys with rich and poor near each other still composed the City's pattern.

The streets of the City were unpaved except near the docks and concentrations of stores. There the medieval practice of laying cobblestones, small round stones set in sand, relieved the mud and dust. Pigs rooted in the street garbage, and packs of dogs harassed the passerby. A few streets had sidewalks paved in brick and were lighted by oil lamps on brackets attached to the walls of houses. At night the watchmen patrolled the streets to look out for the ever-present danger of fire. The City purchased a fire engine to pump water and thirty men organized themselves into a fire company.

Large urban structures were few: the wharves, the shipyards, the churches of the several denominations, the Friends meetinghouse, the synagogue, the open meat and produce markets, the hall where the provincial assembly met, and the new Anglican college established by the governor. In addition the City boasted a long wharf extending from the waterfront into deep water, and a "Broad Way" that ran from the fort at the water's edge to the farm fields beyond town.

A narrow row house, up against the street and sharing a common wall with its neighbors, served the City as its standard building type. Because the carpenters of the city followed the pattern books of London, mean or fashionable, the houses took their lines and forms from the London interpretation of Renaissance

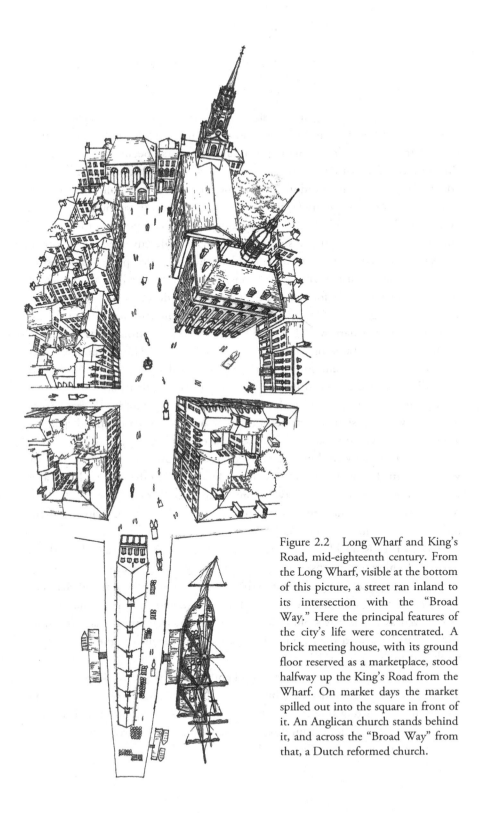

Figure 2.2 Long Wharf and King's Road, mid-eighteenth century. From the Long Wharf, visible at the bottom of this picture, a street ran inland to its intersection with the "Broad Way." Here the principal features of the city's life were concentrated. A brick meeting house, with its ground floor reserved as a marketplace, stood halfway up the King's Road from the Wharf. On market days the market spilled out into the square in front of it. An Anglican church stands behind it, and across the "Broad Way" from that, a Dutch reformed church.

architecture. The Renaissance designs employed a system of symmetrical dimensions and used Roman capitals and arches for windows and doors, setting off the fronts of buildings with pillars and pilasters. Begun in Italy in the fifteenth century with buildings in stone and stucco, the design had been adapted to brick in its London version and in America was followed both in brick and wood. In everyday terms Americans call these building forms "Georgian," "classical," and "Greek revival," depending on the era of construction and the variations within the general style envelope. Such formal styles persisted for a century or more and lent the City a deceptive orderliness.

The standard house offered small rooms that residents used for all manner of work and that sufficed for the needs of a cramped domestic life. The houses ranged from big ones, 25 feet wide, to more common 16- and 18-foot fronts, with some even as narrow as 12 feet. In addition to a few front steps leading to the main door, the building would often be fitted up with slanted wooden covers opening to the basement storage space below. Small rooms, 18 by 18 feet or even 12 by 18, were stacked up one atop the other, the first floor offering one window to the street, a fireplace for cooking and heating, and in the rear corner a narrow winding stair for the second-floor family. In such confined quarters whole families would make their homes, some even taking in a boarder or two.[1]

The small units were but one room deep and most commonly two stories with a cramped attic. The well-to-do added kitchen els in the rear yard, and also enlarged the structure so it was two rooms deep, thereby giving the family three to five rooms in which to house work space, the family and its children, apprentices, servants, and slaves.

Two bedsteads, a table and two chairs, a chest for the husband's tools, perhaps one for clothing and linens, some pots and a fry pan, a pewter plate and mugs were commonplace fittings. Mirrors, tablespoons, knives and forks, and chamber pots were signs of affluence. A privy in the rear yard and an often-contaminated well served as the family's plumbing system. In such cramped quarters tailors and shoemakers plied their trades. It is also well to recall that the City's work week demanded six days' labor.

The high cost of manual construction kept the houses and work spaces small. Timbers had to be hand-sawed by men working in pits or by slow-working windmills, cellars dug by pick and shovel, doors and windows fashioned with hand planes. A mantle surrounding the fireplace and a pillared and pilastered entry might show off a family's wealth.

A People Both Privileged and Enslaved

Immigrants from Europe and slaves from the West Indies made up the overwhelming majority of the City's residents. As an English colony it attracted both Puritans and Anglicans. The Scotch-Irish had left impoverished farms where young people could have little hope of becoming secure tenant farmers on their own. Palatine Germans from the Rhine fled a similar environment, but one made even more intolerable by the religious wars of the seventeenth century and the imperial conflicts of Spain, France, Prussia, and England. The City's slave traders imported slaves from Africa and the West Indies where African prisoners were often taken to "harden," that is to endure and recover from the diseases of Europeans.

Taken in its entirety, the City could be characterized as an assembly of twenty- and thirty-year-olds, a fifth of them being African slaves. Together they represented every branch of Christian faith, and Judaism as well. Perhaps because they were far from Europe, they had abandoned the murderous animosities of seventeenth-century religious wars and instead adopted what would repeat itself as common American practice: prejudice, stereotyping, invidious comparisons, and name calling.

Despite the practice of young white women bearing seven to nine children (slave women hardly reproduced themselves), the City could not grow substantially by natural increase. Contaminated water, spoiled food, and crowded and unsanitary housing combined to "slaughter the innocents." Once a mother stopped nursing her baby, the child faced heavy odds against survival. In contrast to a feeble natural increase, the City gained about 5 percent of its population each year from net migration. That is, despite much traveling up and down the Atlantic coastal towns by young people seeking work and moving inland to find farms, many stayed to try their fortune in the City.

Most merchants did a small trade within the City and to the countryside, or specialized in a few items such as furniture or books. Thus the line between merchant and shopkeeper blurred. Not surprisingly, given the City's dangers to health, widows ran a number of shops and businesses. For most white men in the City a skill was their only source of wealth. If in the old country a young man had mastered a craft, or as a boy had been lucky enough to be apprenticed to a good craftsman, in the City he could expect to make his way to a settled "competence." The tax lists show that in ten years' time one in three residents improved their income.[2] Perhaps four in ten journeymen could expect to marry, raise a family, and move from rented quarters to ownership of a small house in their old age. If, however, a man were unskilled, or as Ben Franklin put it, "bred to country work," he faced a difficult and uncertain life wherein he and his family (if he had one) did well not to starve.

There were boom times when work abounded, times like Queen Anne's War (1702–1713) and the French and Indian War (1754–1763), when privateering brought rich prizes. But hard times followed when prices of export commodities fell steeply and slack trade made work for the unskilled hard to find. Each year the autumn hurricane season in the Caribbean halted the West Indian trade. These were the seasons when the City's almshouse filled with people seeking food and warmth. Even in the best of years, the lower third of the City's

Figure 2.3   College, mid-eighteenth century. In 1750, the town's college consisted of its church, at center, and two identical buildings to either side housing students' and teachers' rooms.

population, the unskilled and the semiskilled, had no chance to rise to the top. They did well to avoid injury and illness and to live past thirty-five years of age. For the widows and the disabled the City offered relief in cash and firewood.

Perhaps because it was a city of young people or perhaps because it was not Europe, the City's residents had a reputation for being saucy and free-spoken, even in the face of their betters. Yet the City stood far from social or even political equality. It possessed a loose but powerful hierarchy. At the top, and dressed accordingly, stood a few English aristocrats and wealthy merchant families. They, and a coterie of merchant associates, physicians, clergymen, lawyers, and teachers, governed the City, their children educated at the new Anglican college.

Divisions among the leaders set in motion a factional politics in which the contending groups sought artisan support. Because elections were by secret ballot and a man could qualify to vote by paying a small fee, electoral contests drew the City's leaders closer to their constituents as the eighteenth century drew on. Political conflict commonly turned around the personality and policies of the royal governor, tax disagreements between those who wished to tax land and issue paper money and those who wanted to tax the merchant's stock, and artisan demands for control of the prices of bread and beer. At times these conflicts exploded into riots, but most of the time the free tax-paying males accepted or ignored royal control.

As in cities across the Atlantic, a new information system had developed to tie together the white males of the City. Both here and in London, a welter of taverns and coffeehouses brought the men together for business transactions, gossip, song, and drink. Occasional street rallies and riots gave expression to the political trends manifested in the tavern conversations. The newspaper, whose columns could connect strangers across town, brought a new element to the city's information exchanges. Imported to America as a part of the business of printing books, pamphlets, and official documents, it opened up a new urban communication system by publishing news, opinion, and advertising notices. Soon printers furnished the City with multiple newspapers and broadsides that were enlisted in factional politics. Harsh language and personal attacks characterized this early journalism. In a novel lawsuit, a newspaper printer in the City had even been absolved for attacking the royal governor, on the grounds that what he printed was true.

Yet, despite this new information system, the social hierarchy of the City sustained deep roots of tradition that resisted change. The majority of the city was not free. Among the white population, women were virtually the property of their husbands. As young women they often served as bound or free servants, and when married their property became their husbands'. Young men commonly worked under articles of apprenticeship and lived in their master's family, subject to his rule. Mariners when at sea labored under a contract that gave all power to the master of the ship. Poor white immigrants often paid for their passage by serving a term of years. Orphans and poor children who had been thrown on the City's charity found themselves sold to families who would agree to care for them in return for their labor.

Although all these practices followed long-extant traditions, they must have made for a city full of chafing and resentments. Such tensions most often took the form of unruly apprentices and servants, and drunken parties in the "bad" part of town. The City, indeed, fostered such a place of unruly taverns, impoverished neighbors, and prostitutes where poverty, frustration, and misery sought company and an outlet.

Domestic tension occasionally reached a high pitch because this was a city of masters who enslaved their fellow human beings, about 3,000 of them. Perhaps just as on the frontier pioneering settlers feared the Amerindians, so in the City whites feared their black slaves. It would not be hard to feel watched and hated. Like their white servant counterparts, some slaves were saucy and hard to govern, and many seem to have sneaked out at night for an occasional party. The common practice of breaking up slave families gave endless trouble and provoked fights when husbands sought their wives.

In 1712 a group of African Americans who complained of "hard usage" rebelled. They set fire to a house and then killed the whites who came to put out the fire. City dwellers also had reports of repeated slave rebellions in the Caribbean and another in South Carolina. "Negro laws" were enacted repeatedly to forbid slaves to own firearms, to be served alcoholic beverages, to walk at night without a lantern, or to gather in groups of more than three.

In 1741 a series of fires in the City set off a wave of fear and a witch hunt to prove a slave conspiracy. The trials resembled the panic and false witnesses of the Salem witch trials, as one New Englander noticed. Whatever the truth may have been, the wave of fear unleashed a ferocity that resembled the massacres of Amerindians on the frontier. Almost two hundred suspect slaves were rounded up under charges that contended they were part of a plot to burn down the City, slaughter its whites, and set up an independent kingdom. Thirteen were burned at the stake, seventeen hanged, two corpses hung on posts in chains so their rotting bodies could serve as a warning to passersby, and 84 slaves were shipped to the Caribbean for hard labor there. Two whites, a man and a woman, named co-conspirators, were also hanged, and seven banished from the City.[3] From such roots the great paradox of American history grew. How did the City of privilege, slavery, fear, and repression become thirty-five years later a leader in the trans-Atlantic experiment in democracy?

3

The Merchant Republic, 1820

Figure 3.1 The City as it appeared in 1820.

THE CITY OF MERCHANTS

The City in the 1820s rushed onward as an American boom town. Despite the destruction and suffering of the Revolutionary War, embargo bankruptcies, and the War of 1812, the City's population had increased to 110,000, a multiplication of six times since 1750. The City's expansiveness rested ultimately on new linkages for overseas and continental shipping and commerce. Ever-shifting European imperial holdings, the colonial revolutions in Latin America, and the connection between the Turkish opium trade and the opening of the port at Canton, China, added fresh channels of trade to the long-established West Indian and European routes. At the same time, the introduction of regularly scheduled sailings from the City to Liverpool and Le Havre intensified trans-Atlantic business.

Continuous warfare against the Amerindian tribes, both in the north and south, opened up the vast eastern third of the continent to American farmers and planters. Wheat and cotton, the staple exports of the nineteenth century, flowed east while immigrants and European manufactured goods traveled west. By 1830, 40,000 immigrants had passed through the City's port bound for the interior, and the City's commission merchants enjoyed an ever-growing trade, sending goods to the west and south to supply storekeepers in the new settlements. Because of the City's close financial ties to English bankers, its merchants became managers of the nation's cotton crop and its stores and shops supplied the planters' slaves with their clothing and tools.

This rush of business with the interior followed new pathways. During the early decades of the nineteenth century, private companies built and operated turnpikes by laying out and grading straight roads for wagons and stagecoaches. Soon thereafter, canal construction and the perfection of the steam-powered river boat connected the City to places as far away as St. Louis and New Orleans via the Great Lakes and the Ohio and Mississippi river systems. Nearer to hand, steam ferries and new bridges connected the City to suburban settlements, while canals brought coal and hay and linked it to the satellite water power sites where new machine-powered textile mills found their beginnings.

By 1820 paper money had earned a deserved reputation for unreliability. "Not worth a Continental" paper dollar was a commonplace phrase. Yet the nation desperately needed capital for all manner of public and private investments. Since banks create money by issuing loans in excess of their deposits, the City and the nation burst forth in banking experiments—a national bank and state-chartered private banks. Absent careful regulation, worthless bank notes and outright fraud fouled the circulation of paper money.[1]

In response, the largest banks instituted the practice of requiring country banks to keep balances with them so that their bank notes would transfer at stable rates. These deposits in time mounted up to a large pool of capital for the City that its banks could loan out at short term. The practice of trading shares of stock in manufacturing corporations and the introduction of the mortgage bond to finance public works further concentrated financial business in the City. During these same years the small holdings of ordinary citizens were bundled together in newly established savings banks.

Yet for all its growing share of the nation's investments, the City remained the puppet of transatlantic capital. Whenever Europeans lessened their American investments to seek more rewarding returns at home, an epidemic of hard times, bankruptcies, price and wage cuts, and unemployment followed.

The Form of the Merchants' City

The City continued in its colonial form of a dense human settlement of wooden and brick houses set one next the other up against the sidewalk; all were contained within a mile from one end of town to the other. Some advance in commodiousness had been achieved since colonial times. Many streets had been paved with stone cobbles and bricks, and large flat stones laid on the sidewalks.

The City pushed outward in a patchwork of subdivisions as fields and woodlots were divided into grids. The grids oriented themselves to the harbor and the river edges and pathways of existing roads. This use of grids of right-angled streets and lots had a long European history. Closer at hand, William Penn's plan for Philadelphia, the Northwest Ordinance of 1787, and the New York Commissioner's Plan of 1811 encouraged the practice. The most powerful determinant, however, derived from the simplicity of surveying made possible by simple right-angled boundaries, and the concomitant certainty of private titles to land. Although land abounded within the municipal boundaries, much of it was held by families who had been favored by colonial connections or had shifted into the hands of a new class of real estate families like John Jacob Astor's. Thus the monopolization of urban land that descended from colonial grants contributed to the formation of a landlord class, a group of people whose income and business rested upon collecting rents.

The development of the City's land, in turn, fostered a multiplication of agents and dealers who stood between home seekers, landowners, and home builders. The hustling real estate business of the day demanded that new streets be laid out in orthogonal grids so that, regardless of inherited land patterns, when a new development was undertaken it would link easily to planned and existing streets. This formalization also facilitated the easy trading of regular-sized parcels. In laying out such plans, the surveyors ignored the natural contours of the land. Because there was money to be made in maximizing the land coverage, little parks and squares like those of contemporary London appeared in only a few new developments.

During the 1820s, the manufacture of gas from coal brought public gaslights to streets to replace their dim oil lamp predecessors. In the same decade, street signs were posted on the second-story walls of corner buildings to indicate the street names. A regular row of trees had been planted along the City's main avenue and, for the well-to-do, omnibus service ran along its length. Churchyards, batteries overlooking the harbor, and an occasional small square in imitation of the ones in London sufficed as the City's parks.

Most of the City's residents walked back and forth to their destinations, facing harassment by the City's hogs as they did so. In 1818 the law allowing the impoundment of roving pigs had been repealed because, in poor neighborhoods, these creatures were regarded as clean-up agents of garbage collection and an important source of a poor family's food. Some butchers in town even farmed hogs as a regular part of their business. Despite mayoral campaigns to round up the free-running hogs, they persisted and multiplied. No one knows their number, but it must have been in the thousands.

A few wealthy families kept horses and carriages, and two-wheeled horse-drawn wagons carried the City's freight, but the years of the horse-dominated city lay a few decades in the future. Porters with handcarts and barrows and peddlers with pushcarts appeared everywhere, while water wagons selling fresh water gave testimony to the town's fragmentary water systems. The civic pride of the era expressed itself in a handsome city hall and large orderly market buildings for fish, meat, and produce.

Much of the City's future physical form depended on its methods of building shops and houses. The standard structure for homes and business continued to be a two-and-a-half-story wooden or brick row house set on a lot 18 to 20 feet wide and up to 100 feet deep. The house ran back from the edge of the sidewalk

Figure 3.2 A commercial street, about 1830. The omnibus was the first method of public transportation in the City. Horses pulled a carriage crammed with passengers along a fixed route down a major commercial street. Most buildings on this street at this time were of brick, owing to fire regulation and the tastes of their wealthy builders, with shops and offices occupying the first two floors. Canvases were drawn taught between hooks on the building facade and posts at the edge of the sidewalk, creating awnings.

40 feet, and was fitted with a raised first floor and a full basement. The fixtures consisted of a cistern to catch the rainwater from the roof, a well with pump, a short exterior front run of steps, a door with a fanlight, and a rear fence and privies. Within the 2,100–2,400 square feet of the structure, the basement held the kitchen and a room used for dining or perhaps a bedroom; above were a first floor of two parlors and an upstairs divided into three or four bedrooms, with additional rooms in the attic for servants and boarders.

As in colonial times, many families occupied this standard house structure as a two-family home, but, in some of the new sections of town, prosperity allowed for its rent or purchase by a single family. A lesser version of the same structure could be divided into two-room "apartments" with kitchen privileges. A three-story version afforded five to eight bedrooms and two kitchens in the basement. The City's prosperity also brought with it a shift from wooden to brick houses, so that by 1830 three-quarters of the houses built that year were of brick. Although brick exterior walls offered little defense to interior wood-framed structures against the multiblock fires that swept the city every thirty years or so, the City passed an ordinance requiring new houses to be built of brick and to have slate roofs. This rule did have the good effect of limiting the damage of the frequent chimney fires that peppered the City.

As the dense little City grew in size, a new social and economic geography began to emerge. New construction advanced at the fringes while, in the old areas of town, houses were cut up. Because the landlords had no legal obligation to maintain their buildings, living conditions in such low-rent buildings deteriorated rapidly. At the same time, the new scale of business and new forms of specialization began to alter some old neighborhoods. Merchants and some shopkeepers turned their former work-and-residence structures into all-business places. Thus, streets of merchants, often with a scattering of new large three- and four-story buildings, sprang up to make a new business district, a proto-downtown. Along the shore, shipbuilders expanded their yards, and new four- and five-story warehouses began to appear next the wharves.

Some streets of sellers of imported goods organized themselves into incipient retail strips; to replace the discomforts of the boardinghouse, a few large hotels sprang up on the edge of good neighborhoods. Some of these even offered guests a single room to themselves. Two brothers from Switzerland, a pastry chef and a wine importer, opened a coffeehouse and soon transformed it into a novelty for America, a French restaurant. In such a place diners could order from a menu

Figure 3.3   At the harbor, 1820. Nineteenth-century brigs, quite a bit higher than all construction in town except for church steeples, docked at a crowded waterfront to unload their cargos of molasses, turpentine, and manufactures of Europe and the Far East.

whatever dishes they wished, and they ate at a private table covered with a white tablecloth. Theirs was a formidable advance over the fixed offering of the boardinghouse and tavern. The Swiss partners, like Thomas Jefferson, even tried without much success to get their customers to eat salads.[2]

By 1830 the City had by no means assumed the functional business or residential geography of a modern American city, though these lineaments appeared in embryonic form. The segregation of classes, immigrants, and African Americans into uniform neighborhoods had hardly begun. Except in the very newest and most expensive areas, the working classes, tradesmen, and immigrants lived side by side with more wealthy and long-settled families. Church congregations formed cultural units, but did not compose exclusive neighborhoods. Moreover, such was the small extent of the city that people could easily walk about to maintain their connections of kin and friendship. One exception to the mixed residential pattern had begun to appear in 1830. A few of the wealthy old established families began to withdraw from the commonplace City into small upper-class enclaves.[3]

Three different levels of enterprise characterized the building business: one-man operators, master carpenters, and large-scale developers. An army of small independent builders constructed hundreds of dwellings. Each year these craftsmen would build two to three houses to offer for sale, hiring by the day the plasterers, slaters, and masons as they required their services.

The master carpenters stood as a class above the small-time builders. The masters assumed the new ways we associate today with general contractors. These individuals took on strips of lots and whole blocks to run up houses for rent and for sale. Whereas in colonial times the master builder and his journeymen would work as a team—the journeymen being paid at an established rate for a day's work—now the masters paid by the hour and sought to use as few journeymen as possible. The additional skills they required they now hired on fixed-price contracts. By such means the master carpenters enlarged the scope of their business and simultaneously destroyed the old craft training and mutual responsibilities that had formerly prevailed.

A few entrepreneurs managed to transform themselves into large-scale developers. These men worked through another new institution, the real estate broker, to arrange contracts for large tracts of fringe land. On occasion they drained swampy areas or leveled hills to make substantial subdivisions of houses for rent or for sale.

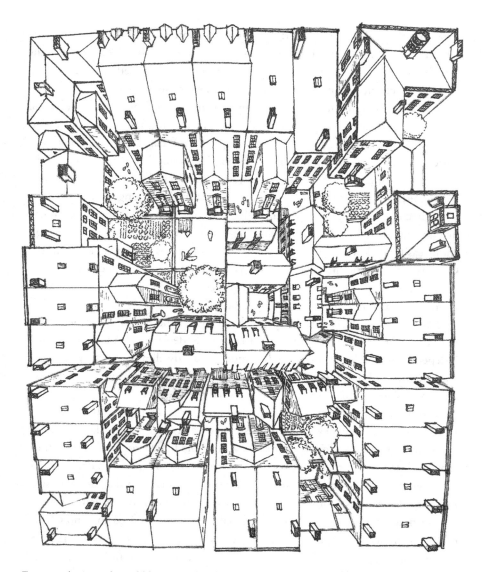

Figure 3.4 A residential block, 1820. At this time each block generally housed residents of all classes as well as some craftsmen's workshops. Many still featured small gardens and open spaces. The grandest homes on the block were clustered at the corners and were modeled after those of Georgian and Regency London. In the City the style was termed Federalist, after the dominant political party in the Northeast from the Revolution until the War of 1812. They were mostly of brick, though a few were built of stone, and often featured wrought-iron balconies, multiple rooms for entertainment, and quarters for domestic help. Other homes facing the exterior of the block had been subdivided into smaller rental quarters, while those on the interior, often of wood, were almost exclusively home to laborers.

Big or small, builders shared a common discipline in the capital market. America was an underdeveloped nation, short on capital. Money to acquire land and raise buildings could only be had on short terms. A builder could reduce his up-front costs by not purchasing a lot but instead building on a ground lease. These commonly ran twenty-one years before the land and structure reverted to the lessor. Mortgages ran for one to five years at 6 percent. In a common deal, the purchaser put up one-fifth of the total price and paid 20 percent of the balance each year. If a buyer could put half the price down at the outset, then an eight- to ten-year mortgage would be possible. Cooperative building societies with their amortizing mortgages, the common form the United States government adopted in the 1930s, had yet to appear, and, absent the ability of banks in the 1830s to loan on long terms, private investors, merchants, and shopkeepers made up the market of mortgage lenders.

This discipline of speculative land prices and short-term capital forced a uniform process upon the City. New construction could be profitable to all parties only if it catered to the upper half of the housing market. No secure profits could be expected from attempts to build for ordinary working families, or for the poor. For these people, the majority of the City's residents, existing houses were cut up by landlords into boardinghouses and one- and two-room "apartments"; families had to crowd into small quarters to find living space.

An Uneasily Prosperous People

The continuing general homogeneity of the City's residential geography, coupled with the persistence of building styles that resembled those of colonial days, masked powerful economic trends that were transforming long-established ways of organizing work. The master carpenters led the way soon after the Revolution. Formerly, theirs had been a benevolent association of masters and journeymen. Once a year the association established the price for a journeymen's day of work. Now new tactics evolved out of bidding on construction jobs. The master bid by totaling his estimates of journeymen's days needed, then adding a small percentage as a contractor's fee. This addition was not shared with the crew. Moreover, if the bid succeeded, the master tried to substitute as many laborers and unskilled men as possible instead of hiring a full complement of journeymen and apprentices. Boom times advantaged those who found ways to reduce the proportion of skilled workers in their businesses. The journeymen carpenters responded by leaving the master's association and establishing one of their own, a trade union.

As early as 1799 a typographic union formed to protect typesetters and printers from their employers. Tailors, shoemakers, and stonecutters unionized, too, and soon the English and German stocking weavers, Irish linen weavers, and Scots rug weavers added their unions to the growing craft list. Many of these unions used a particular tavern in the City as a communications hub, and some even maintained "rats lists" of employers who paid below-union rates. In the years from 1827 to the depression of 1837, the unions in town formed all-craft, united unions to press for a ten-hour day and a six-day week.

The ten-hour movement expressed the prevailing ideology of the times. It called up a vision of a white man's republic, a city composed of citizens who would be rewarded for their work by becoming independent proprietors in time, with their own shops and lists of customers. The men called for public education for their children and a limited ten-hour day for themselves so that they might read to better themselves and spend a little time with their families. Far from announcing themselves as a separate class, they asserted that as citizens they were just as good as the wealthy, the "aristocrats" and the "exclusives," as they called them. Indeed, they shared the same free-enterprise economic agenda with those so privileged. The City's unions in 1830 spoke the language of Tom Paine and Thomas Jefferson, who imagined a nation of independent proprietors.

Whenever the union men organized for a strike, however, they faced the danger of being arrested under long-established criminal conspiracy laws. Thus, from the very outset of the transformation of American work, those that organized faced a deep injustice rooted in the law, an injustice only partially remedied a century later. The relations among masters and journeymen and apprentices were set forth in contracts recognized by civil law. These documents functioned much as a contract for a purchase might. Yet when labor conflicts over the performance of these contracts turned to walkouts and strikes, they were met with criminal laws with consequences of fines and imprisonment. (By contrast, during the 1820s states abolished the practice of imprisonment for debt.)

So, beneath the economic boom and amid the shouts and slogans for the independent man, there emerged whole classes of city dwellers who had no access to customers and no independence as proprietors. They were a new class of wage workers, poor men, African American freemen, children, and women.

As in colonial times, poor men performed the City's tasks as laborers, porters in the markets, loaders and unloaders of ships at the wharves, wood sawyers, and hod carriers. All these stood unprotected from the physical severities of the weather and the seasons, from the slack time when the Erie Canal froze, and from the uncertainties of international shipping. To these laborers also should be added the house servants, laundresses, and many men and women who did odd jobs for shopkeepers and families, plus the male and female street sellers. A study in 1829 estimated that rent and fuel demanded two-thirds of these workers' earnings.[4]

The new economy added another layer to the laboring classes, that of the semiskilled. These workers knew but part of a task or craft, and most of them worked in rooms whose rent they had to pay out of their earnings. Others of this group worked as machine tenders in the new suburban textile mills. Within the City proper, the largest proportion of this group did piecework, laboring at home on shoe and clothing materials furnished by their employers. One garment firm had 600 women on its lists of home-based pieceworkers. To these semiskilled workers should be added the very large number of skilled journeymen craftsmen who would never enjoy a chance at proprietorship.

As always, the stresses of economic and social change bore most heavily on the least-defended members of society, the African Americans, the children, and the women. During the Revolution, the British army's recruiting and the general confusion had enabled a number of slaves to become free. Then, bit by bit, the northern states abolished the laws legalizing human property. Yet so deep ran American prejudices that, just as white men were winning universal suffrage for themselves, they passed laws to deny the same privilege to blacks.

Within the City and underneath its layers of white citizens, however, the African American freemen had successfully fashioned a community of their own. They built churches, established schools and Masonic lodges, and a few managed to succeed with independent businesses. In the decade of the 1820s, African Americans continued to be excluded from skilled crafts and many of the City's licensed trades. Over the years, immigrants and white country folk forced more and more of them out of domestic work. They were allowed, however, to monopolize the role of "tubmen," the laborers who dug out the City's privies and carried off the night soil. The hostility of white men, to some extent fueled by competition for jobs, ran deep. Often gangs of boys would attack blacks and set dogs upon them as they walked the City's streets. When African Americans wished to celebrate the abolition of slavery by the state of New York on July 4, 1827, they cautiously postponed their exercises to the next day lest they be attacked by liquored-up Independence Day crowds.[5]

The shifts in family work routines and the decay of the institution of apprenticeship left many of the City's children exposed to long hours and ill-paid work. As late as 1830, the City lacked a unified and comprehensive public grammar school system. Church-supported schools and schools managed by a large public charitable organization offered primary education to boys and girls who could be spared from work to attend. Roughly one-quarter of the City's population was five to fifteen years of age. Of this group of 27,500, one half attended school, the other half worked, and some mix of both groups formed into boys' gangs that stole and harassed.

For many women, conditions had deteriorated since colonial times. The laborer's wife had made her home in a cramped room in the eighteenth century, but now, with boom time's pressure on rents, the rooms shrank. Formerly, the wives and apprenticed children had been part of a proprietary production system. Or widows, if they had some space, could maintain themselves by taking in boarders. Now, with the pinch on space and low-wage work, women could not support themselves on their earnings; their wages stood at one-half the men's. Many were driven to periodic charity as in the past, and it has been estimated that 10 percent of the City's females took up prostitution for some period in their lives.[6]

For a brief time during the late 1820s and early 1830s the white man's City of merchants, artisans, and wage workers prospered and seemed to European observers to validate the American experiment in democracy. In such a society, however, always hungry for credit, the alternations of boom and bust in the Atlantic economy to which the City was tethered could bring disaster as well as prosperity. Like the nation as a whole, the City's internal economic and social processes threatened to destroy its civil peace, if not its formal political structures.

4

THE CITY OVERWHELMED, 1860

Figure 4.1 The City as it appeared in 1860.

The City and the Wealth of Two Continents

There are decades in the nation's experience when events come on so fast and from so many directions that they overwhelm accepted wisdom and exceed the capacity of social and political innovators to respond effectively. The accelerating pace of business and the growth of the City in the years from 1840 to 1860 both rested on extraordinary events. Gold from California and Australia and periodic surges of capital from Europe formed deep pools of wealth that funded the building of the northeastern and midwestern railroad and telegraph network and supported a vastly expanded coastwise and oceanic fleet. The new wealth settled half the continent with farms and plantations, raised factories, stores, and offices, and laid down waterworks and street railways. A succession of inventions from the sewing machine to rotary presses and the multiplication of power-driven tools began a process of continuous industrialization. Such a tumult of events propelled the City's extraordinary development, although its old forms persisted.

Once again overseas events shaped the City's experience. In Europe a succession of crop failures drove thousands from their villages and farms. The French and the Germans called these times the "hungry forties," and in both nations the decade ended with failed liberal revolutions. In Ireland the potato blight brought starvation. It has been estimated that a million died there in the decade after 1845, and a million more fled to the United States. Unfortunately for the Irish poor, Ben Franklin's truth still prevailed that those "bred to country work" would face hardship when they came to the City.

The Shape of the Antebellum City

In 1860 the City's population count stood at 400,000, and 80,000 more lived in its satellite city across the harbor. Nearby, too, small factory and farm villages probably added 20,000 more inhabitants to the commonplace rhythms of the city. Some 40 percent of the City's population had been born overseas: 100,000 came from Ireland, 40,000 from Germany, and 20,000 from England and Scotland. The number of Irish women exceeded that of the men by 10,000, thereby creating a huge pool of domestic service and factory labor.

Such a rush of population caused the City to grow at the fastest rate in its entire history, three and a half times in thirty years. Building continued along the general eastward pathway established with the City's first settlement by straddling the harbor and the narrow river to the north. The old streets grew ever more crowded, while new building crossed the river on the north side and spread out toward the farms on the east end of town. Across the harbor to the south the large satellite city boomed, in part by repeating the urban fabric of the City proper and in part by becoming a special place of heavy waterfront industry: sugar refining, ironworks, shipyards, and kerosene refining. In the nearby countryside, a number of farming villages prospered with the addition of villas and the cottages of steam railroad commuters to the downtown. Within the City, vast areas of commonplace living stretched north and east to make a kind of architectural pudding of mixed rows of houses, shops, barns, and small factories.

The decades since 1840 had brought major additions to the City's infrastructure. Some of these improvements merely facilitated the enlargement of the City without changing the arrangement of its buildings: horsecars, public water, gas, and telegraph lines. Together these new underlying elements created the public-transportation, hard-wired, and piped city whose engineering persisted for the next one hundred years. Other additions, including the steam railway, new methods of business, elaboration of the enclave of the wealthy, and the invention of the cheap tenement, altered the economic and social structure of the City.

The business of the harbor flourished and piers and warehouses multiplied with the ever-growing traffic of steam and sail. Private gas companies lit the streets, houses, and businesses, and, as their service grew, their large gasometers rose next to the coal wharves to give the City a new industrial landmark. Steam ferries linked the City to its satellite across the harbor, and tugs and barges brought coal, hay, lumber, and stone to its wharves. Long-distance and international sailings became everyday affairs.

The introduction of street railway cars pulled by teams of horses opened up quantities of fringe land beyond the limits of an easy hour's walk so that new construction could continue in the familiar row house patterns, thereby keeping the City's non-slum density at about 6–7 persons per house. The horsecar also advanced a new urban social pattern, because even its modest fare sorted riders from pedestrians. Middle-class families commuted from home to the workplace on public transportation, while most residents could afford only to walk. Horsecars and ferries carried the most passengers, while the railroads accommodated the

Figure 4.2 Ironworks, 1860. To the left were blast furnaces, powered by coal, where iron ore was transformed into pig iron. The pig iron was then moved into the adjacent foundry, where it was melted again and cast into a variety of products.

more distant and affluent families. By such means the City spread into a now-familiar pattern of an urban core surrounded by residential sectors and districts of industry.

The steam railroad and magnetic telegraph carried goods, passengers, and news from city to city at an unprecedented speed, thereby accelerating both the volume of business transactions and the speed at which capital could flow. City dwellers have long been thought to walk and talk faster than their country cousins, but now a modern urban pace set in. The steam trains at first were required to locate their stations and yards at the edges of settlement, both because of fear of fire and because in the early years railroads could not afford the price of center city land. Yet from the beginning, they contributed to the uglification of the City with smoke, noise, and accidents.

The steam railroads also permanently altered the form of the City by adding industrial corridors to the well-established ones at portside. Next to the railroad yards and the railroad's radiating lines factories and warehouses located, to get access for their materials and shipments. In time these lines expanded to form the pie-shaped industrial sectors of the metropolis, a pattern finally made permanent by zoning legislation.

The telegraph likewise initiated its own uglification—streets lined with poles and wires whose intrusions would continue with electrification and cable networks. In the years before 1861 the City had been served with private mail delivery companies, but in that year Congress established letter delivery as a national monopoly. Thereafter, the uniformed postman and telegraph boy began their long careers as the human embodiments of modern communications.

Fear of fires and epidemics drove the City to undertake an enormous investment in a municipal water system. In the process, cast-iron pipes replaced the leaky old elm pipes of private water companies. Unfortunately, when the City offered fresh water, it did not require its installation in every dwelling. The municipal pipes ran under the street, but the landowner had to pay for the connection to his property. For many years following the installment of the new 1846 system, slumlords refused the expense and forced their tenants to rely on the public hydrant and backyard privy.

Because the municipal waterworks required such a large capital investment for reservoirs, pumping stations, and service pipes, it alone among the infrastructure initiatives went forward as a unified network. All the other utilities were piecemeal installations that grew as a patchwork of private operations:

ferries, railroads, gas lighting, and horsecar lines. Midcentury Americans held an unshakable faith in the rewards of the private market, so that the City parceled out franchises bit by bit and left it to the customers to negotiate the ill-fitting routes and schedules and varying standards as best they could. Subsequently, private investors and public regulators labored for more than a century to reconfigure the City's utilities into unified systems.

The burst of growth after 1830 began a process of class and functional specialization of the City's land. Most of the areas of the city continued the old form of mixed streets of houses, shops, small factories, and stables, but three specialized areas appeared: the business district, the warren of poverty, and the enclave of the wealthy.

A well-defined area of high-rent land and intense commercial activity established the core of the City. In 1860 it consisted of blocks of five-story warehouses, four- or five-story merchant countinghouses and wholesale offices, banks and law offices, hotels, and retail stores. The City had never before witnessed whole blocks of stores, some large and luxurious, others small narrow storefronts. The 1860s stores were not the artisan and importers' shops scattered among the merchants' homes and warehouses of former times, but a distinct area in its own right. As retail outlets, the stores gathered up the products of the City's factories and wholesale houses; only a few items were made on the premises. They also arranged themselves according to their customers' pocketbooks: luxury "palace stores" on one street, clusters of inexpensive wares on another.

Some of these business center structures continued the older pattern of stone and brick facing, but since the 1840s a new material had come into popularity: cast iron. Molded into pillars, pilasters, posts, stairs, and window frames, it allowed the facades of these four- and five-story buildings to offer large glass windows to light the interior and to display wares to the passerby. In these years of disastrous fires that consumed whole acres of the City, it was hoped that the cast-iron buildings would be fireproof. The wooden interior flooring, partitions, and roof, however, nullified the cast-iron benefit because, as the fire heated the iron and firemen's hoses played upon it, the iron cracked and the whole structure failed. Subsequent to the Civil War, an economic boom and a new invention called forth eight- and ten-story "elevator" office buildings.

Despite bigger houses, bigger stores, bigger warehouses, bigger ships, the explosive growth of the City brought hardship and disaster to many. The small

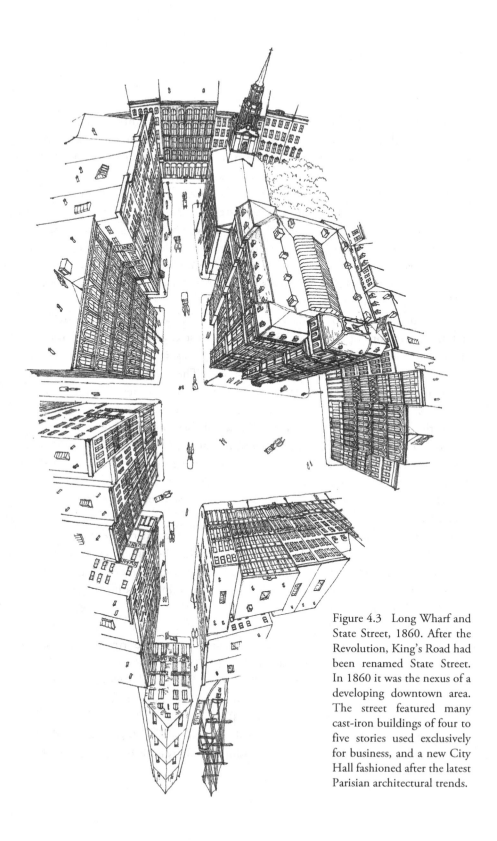

Figure 4.3 Long Wharf and State Street, 1860. After the Revolution, King's Road had been renamed State Street. In 1860 it was the nexus of a developing downtown area. The street featured many cast-iron buildings of four to five stories used exclusively for business, and a new City Hall fashioned after the latest Parisian architectural trends.

wooden houses and cramped rooms of the poor of former times multiplied and divided and divided and subdivided to form a whole quarter of concentrated poverty. Despite the building booms of the forties and fifties, the owners of urban land and the home builders held forth only the meanest offerings for the waves of unskilled immigrants from Ireland and Germany. The commonest landowner's response sought to turn a profit from the clustering of small rents. Landlords and sublandlords divided up old houses and their basements into single- and two-room apartments in which whole families (some with boarders) crowded. Weekly and two-week rentals were common, and in hard times tenants had no way to escape the rent collector but to skip out with their few pieces of furniture.

The era between 1840 and 1860 was a time of extraordinary ingenuity and useful invention. Alas, in the list of new designs, there appeared the unwelcome invention of the purpose-built tenement, a special building for poor people. In this case, three- to five-story block buildings with windows in the front and the rear filled the entire lot, leaving only ten feet to the rear for privies. As a result, many lived in windowless interior rooms. The poor themselves added their mite to the mean efforts of the City's landlords. In the spaces behind old buildings and in the rough spots at the outer edges of new building the poor threw up shacks and shanties. Together, the tenement infill, the old-building subdivisions, and the shanties created a dense warren of poverty.

Its main area stretched back from the old harborside and sailors' boardinghouses to form a crescent along the harbor and to the edges of the new business center. Contemporaries recognized it as a distinct environment of ill-maintained buildings, bad ventilation, dirty rooms, and unsanitary basement yards and streets piled with the garbage and trash that threatened the residents' health and nourished some of the City's 10,000 pigs.

In imitation of sanitarians in England and Europe, reformers began to gather statistics on the location of deaths within the City. They reasoned that damp basement rooms and trash-laden and ill-ventilated apartments helped spread the periodic epidemics of yellow fever and cholera. They began to speak of an urban environment as the nursery of disease, and called for alternate forms of construction and publicly enforced cleaning as the means to contain epidemics.

The City's health officer even proposed a sensible remedy: If a landlord failed to keep his building clean, the City would impose a fine and also send in a clean-up crew and charge the landlord for the service. Such a commonsense proposal exceeded the bounds of acceptable municipal initiative, because contemporaries had fixed upon individual morality as the cause of filth and dirt and had established the sacredness of private property as the barrier to public intrusion.

Yet these early observations and proposals brought forth phrases that would be repeated over and over again: "It is often said one half of the world does not know how the other half lives."[1] Perhaps this was an empty phrase even then, because many of the rich seemed to know well what was going on. A transit promoter put forth a proposal that would be repeated for the next half-century. Not wages but cheap transportation, he said, would relieve the poor: "We might enlarge upon the misery and vice and disease engendered by the overcrowding of the lower end of our city. Model lodging houses and sanitary regulations are excellent in their way, but the prime remedy lies in facilitating the dispersion of population by easy and cheap methods of transit."[2]

A number of the wealthy continued the withdrawal from the commonplace City districts that had begun in an earlier generation. They advanced along new streets at the eastern edge of town, and a few even settled in Gothic-style villas in small suburban villages on the north side of the City.

In addition, near to the new retail downtown and growing out of the earlier enclave of the wealthy, a mixed district of fashion and civic institutions began to take shape. Large town houses for the wealthy were interspersed with civic organizations such as St. Patrick's Cathedral, Temple Emanuel, Union League, Columbia College, and the Lenox Library.[3]

Within the City the new wealth and numbers afforded a larger exclusive enclave and the construction of more pretentious houses. Their row houses grew from three to four stories, and like the tenements of the poor filled much of a 25-by-100-foot lot. The new Italianate and Gothic styles brought forth more elaborate ornamentation than that of the previous century. Here, too, cast iron sprouted forth in fancywork fences, stairs, and front balconies. Parlors expanded from single to double, with tea rooms tacked on behind. Marble fireplaces replaced wood, and the new luxuries of steam heat, running hot and cold water, baths, and toilets became standard for the rich. Developers of upscale blocks often set aside a small square in imitation of London fashions, and public gardens and parks were planned as devices to raise land values at the edge of town.

Figure 4.4 A suburban house, 1860. When the City began to annex neighboring towns in the mid-nineteenth century and extend the provision of water, and as other towns developed their own public services, many middle-class households began to mimic the bourgeois trends of an earlier generation. On the urban fringe they built homes in the eclectic styles then fashionable: Greek revival, Italianate, Gothic, and Second Empire.

A City of Immigrants

In the 1860 City, ethnic organizations flourished; churches, schools, athletic and singing clubs, fire companies, and militia units all organized themselves according to race and national origin, but these were not yet set in spatial patterns. In ordinary neighborhoods the native born and the immigrants mingled in a rough sorting that varied according to employment specialties. The American-born Yankees dominated commerce at all levels from clerk to merchant, such that the merchants became new commuters from their wealthy enclaves and the clerks in stores and offices walked to work from old homes situated on the edge of the business district. The American-born dominated in skilled crafts like jewelry making and printing, trades that kept them near the center, but their specialties in machining, metal working, and prefabricated doors, stairs, and other millwork created additional clusters of industry near the lumber wharves and the waterside foundries.

English immigrants likewise concentrated in commerce, printing, and textiles, thereby contributing to the mix in such neighborhoods of the City. Germans gathered around furniture, cabinetmaking, musical instruments, apparel, grocery stores, butcher shops, and brewing and distilling. In so doing, they both concentrated in a few places and scattered throughout the City. In contrast, the Irish peasant immigrants had to begin their lives in the City at the least-skilled levels. Thirty percent worked in domestic service, 15 percent as laborers. Some managed as grocers and saloon keepers, and many others found niches making cheap shoes and clothing.

Despite fraud and chicanery of every sort, those holding urban land—syndicates of mill builders, railroad promoters, innovating retailers, and international bankers—made millions. Thousands of others also rode the boom times in the City as storekeepers, craftsmen, manufacturers, wholesale merchants, agents of all kinds, and doctors and lawyers. By hard work and small savings these white city dwellers managed to find a comfortable living and a respectable home.

Since most of the City's manufacturing and storekeeping went forward in small workshop rooms and narrow stores scattered everywhere, an occupational and ethnic patchwork appeared on almost every block. The waves of new immigrants and the severe depression of 1837–1842 set back the ten-hour movement; people working the standard twelve-hour day and six-day week wanted to live near their work. Scattered work locations thereby established the City's mixing of natives and immigrants. In most of the City, except in the warrens of poverty and the enclave of the wealthy, the class mix of one block much resembled another's.

The banner of the white man's republic continued to fly over the City where many believed that, if you were a citizen, one man was as good as the next. It was a heady assumption and it seemed to set people free to imagine a host of social innovations. On any given night in the City a person could hear a lecture on the abolition of slavery, the dangers of Catholicism, the failings of immigrants, the need for temperance, the necessity for free land and labor unions, calls for new freedoms and rights for women, and the need for the alternatives of communitarian settlements and socialism. Popular preachers even asserted that good men and sinners both could communicate directly with God.

These were exciting times, full of both hope and intolerance. Never before had so many participated in elections, and never had government been so close to its citizens. Elite dominance in politics, the rule in former times, gave way to white men's democratic assertions. Successive reforms dispersed municipal authority into nests of boards and ward committees, and the common man gained public office. The City became, as it would remain for decades, a shopkeeper's and artisan's republic. Wealthy men continued to be chosen for mayor, but below that office sat men of greater variety. At one moment in the 1850s, the City's Board of Aldermen seated a tobacconist, a saloon keeper, a stonecutter, a butcher, a saddler, a fruit vendor, a fishmonger, a chair maker, and a livery stable proprietor—small men seeking small fortunes.

Representation and participation, however, failed to manage the turmoil within the City. The white man's republic presided over waves of racial and religious prejudice. Though its government was secular, the City had long been a Protestant town, and now it had to learn to accept thousands of Catholic Irish and Germans. The rush of immigrants called forth the fears and animosities of nativism, while the opponents of slave liberation fed the angers of white racism. Moreover, these organized prejudices rested on top of the daily conflicts and frustrations of a City of day labor, piecework, and unregulated exploitation.

Thus, beneath the formal politics of City, state, and nation, there surged a violent politics of gangs, fire company rivalries, and riots that often continued for days at a time. Essentially powerless in their everyday circumstances, native and immigrant gangs fell back on the tenuous social order of maintaining their turf, keeping the blocks around their clubhouse or saloon under their control. In the process, they terrorized pedestrians, covered fences and walls with graffiti, and set fires to lure their rivals. Although the daily fistfights and drunken brawls often led to little more, year after year serious rioting broke out, finding targets that matched the politics of the day. Anti-Catholic mobs burned a convent and destroyed a Catholic church by cannon fire; a weavers' strike turned into a three-day riot. Orange-against-Green mobs drove Irish immigrants from their homes. Although the City installed a regular uniformed police force in the 1850s, it lacked sufficient power to contain the largest riots. For these the Mayor had to summon the militia, whose companies often favored the rioters.

In these frequent outbursts the crowds were encouraged by the rhetoric of those in positions of power. Many voters felt that "their America" was, and ought to remain, a Protestant nation. Anti-Catholic riots fed on these municipal and anti-immigrant politics that flourished in the 1840s and 1850s. The most continuous and severe riots, however, stemmed from the deepest cleavage in American society—slavery, Negrophobia, and the common belief that the United States was a white man's republic. Much of the City's commerce rested upon trade with the South and its manufacture of cotton textiles. "Cotton Whigs," political leaders who viewed antislavery as anathema, fed the prejudice of the streets. Neighborhoods, churches, and schools of African Americans suffered continuing attack by mobs whose frequency and intensity increased as the antislavery movement gained ground.

The Civil War did not extinguish these animosities. Instead it fed the accumulated anger. A very deep depression in 1857 that left thousands unemployed and dependent on City relief for fuel and food was followed by steep wartime price inflation. Many of the City's leaders opposed the war and spoke actively against it. For those without money to purchase exemptions, it was a rich man's war and a poor man's fight. As a result, when in 1863 a national draft for soldiers began, the City exploded into four days of rioting. It was both a class and race explosion, with days of looting and lynching. The targets were stores, antislavery newspapers, and African Americans. Blacks were hunted down, strung from lampposts and burned. Hundreds fled the city as best they could. The dispersed and scattered nature of the City's class and racial pattern enabled the violent attacks to appear all over town.[4] Troops fresh from the victory at Gettysburg had to be rushed into the City by train to restore order. A clever President quieted the City by a subtle manipulation of its antiwar politicians. He appointed them to offices where they held the responsibility for restoring order. It proved a winning maneuver, but the riots left an enduring scar. The unruly behavior of the City during these decades realized the deep-seated antiurban prophecies of Jefferson and Tocqueville. Now, as in Europe after the 1848 revolutions, the poor, the warren dwellers, became "the dangerous classes."

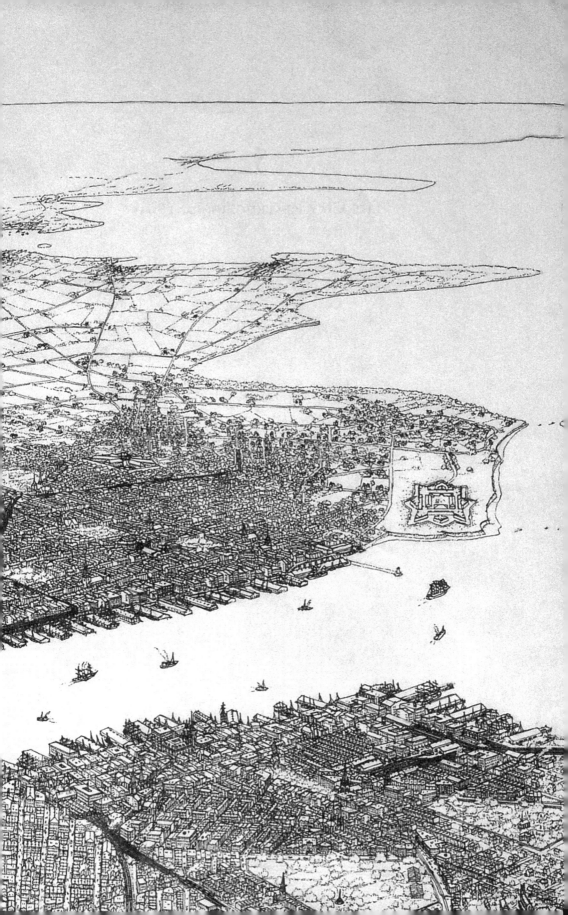

5

The City Restructured, 1895

Figure 5.1 The City as it appeared in 1895.

The Industrial Metropolis

Swept forward by intensifying industrialization and by the flood of young rural and village Europeans seeking a new livelihood, the City, like all the major cities of Europe and the United States, continued its unprecedented rate of growth. By 1895 it was one of sixteen in the world to have exceeded one million inhabitants. By the force of its commercial, financial, and industrial institutions it came to dominate a large region of the nation.

Several striking changes in buildings and land use gave the city a new form and appearance at this time: the downtown built upward as its offices and stores stretched from five and ten stories to ten and twenty; five-story factories and warehouses became commonplace, and workrooms spread to include whole floors of these structures. A few took a new fireproof form of steel and concrete construction.

The Form of the Industrial Metropolis

These new structure types were fostered by the rapid multiplication of a new institution: the private business corporation. The private corporation of the 1890s evolved from the experience of the railroads. By the nineties it had settled into patterns of stock and bond capital formation and management organization that allowed large mechanized production processes to be sustained. Supported by the abundant financial resources, the City's pools of immigrant labor, and the regional dominance of its port and railroads, corporate mechanized production refashioned the City's geography. Manufactures of all kinds, and their warehousing and jobbing support, spread outward from the edge of the office and retail downtown along the railroad corridors to the metropolitan edge. Here old products like cordage, boxes, flour, printing, railroad cars, and locomotives joined new products like electrical machinery, cast-iron stoves, drugs, telephones, plumbing supplies, meatpacking, cigarettes, and candy. New steel, rubber, ceramic, cement, chemical, and oil refining installations settled at the metropolitan fringe where land was cheap and rail service abundant. The outer heavy industries established satellite towns of their own, the mills being surrounded by workers' housing: the skilled men in little detached houses, the unskilled in tenements. The extraordinarily successful Singer Manufacturing Corporation demonstrated the new corporate urban pattern of sales and manufacturing. It built a skyscraper in the City's center for its commuting workers and located its sewing machine factory ten miles away in an industrial satellite. Later, during the 1920s, these rail-industrial spines became fixed elements of the urban landscape when zoning laws designated the areas for exclusive industrial use.

At the center of the industrial spiderweb the municipality added infrastructure that supported the central concentration of the metropolis. It financed the filling of the marshes in a broad area beyond the western bridge from the downtown. In addition to laying out new streets, it set aside a large area of the new land as a country-style park in the midst of the new neighborhood. A group of wealthy bankers and real estate speculators established a Methodist university next the park. Located as it was, convenient to the downtown, it quickly filled with substantial row houses. By 1895 the neighborhood had become a residential den for the City's professionals.

Elsewhere, in a band around the City, the current fashion in country parks spurred the addition of three new parks to serve as citizen escapes from the dense living of their streets. These, in conjunction with two earlier rural-style cemeteries, provided the City's inhabitants with moments of the pastoral landscape experience that had heretofore been the special privilege of wealthy estate owners.

Most of the streets of the City remained unpaved gravel ways. But in the downtown and next to factories and warehouses, the abutters repaved many streets. At first the new paving had been set between and along the horsecar tracks, but in time the practice spread. Belgian blocks, small rectangular flat granite stones, replaced the former round and bumpy cobbles and the more fragile bricks. In the country parks and along a few fashionable boulevards where carriage owners showed off their equipage, the City carefully laid out macadam roads and a few asphalt roadways.[1]

The generation and distribution of electric power during these years intensified the uses and land values of the downtown. The new electric-powered streetcars were larger than the horsecars they replaced and traveled faster, thus lengthening the commuting lines to the City's center. Electrification, however, could do nothing to relieve the City's downtown traffic jams. The large streetcars had to wait their turn in the daily jams along with the horse-drawn wagons and the crowds of pedestrians. It was estimated that for every 100 hours a teamster, horses, and wagon worked in the City, they had to spend 29.2 hours in waiting

Figure 5.2   Park, 1895. At the end of the nineteenth century the City was festooned with public parks. The largest were dotted with man-made ponds, small pavilions, and winding paths that gave ample opportunity for picturesque views and recreation. Flora was imported from around the globe to add color and touches of the exotic.

and traffic congestion.[2] In response to this downtown congestion, the private streetcar monopoly constructed an elevated line around the City's center that linked the two major railroad stations in a line that stretched along the harbor and extended north into what had become a working-class area.

Elevateds, though quick and handy, were not popular. They darkened the streets beneath them and ruined the quiet and comfort of the abutting buildings. Many urged an alternative, the construction of a subway that would follow the example of London. Tunnels under the streets, however, cost millions to construct, so that no private company could afford to build one. Like waterworks and major land fillings, subways required public capital. The city of Boston built a short pioneer line in 1897 and leased the tunnel to a private traction company. Such a method became for a time the municipal model, making it possible to move ever more shoppers and workers in and out of the City's center.

The telegraph had been improved by the introduction of automatic printers and teletypewriters, replacing the notoriously cranky services of telegraphers.

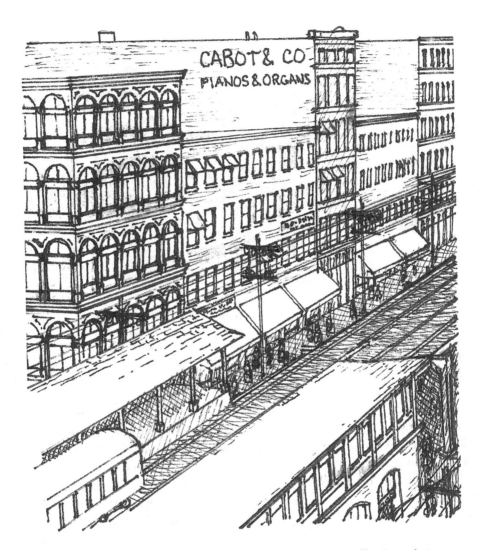

Figure 5.3 The el, 1895. Downtown streetcars became stalled in traffic. One solution was the construction of an elevated line that wound through downtown and then out to the residential northeast. Though cheaper to build than a subway, the elevated line brought darkness and additional noise and pollution to the street, and blocked the view of retailers' storefronts.

The national communications monopoly, Western Union, was soon joined by Bell's telephone enterprise. By 1895 the phone had proved itself a useful instrument for business, but only 10 percent of residences had been connected for service.[3] In most neighborhoods the phone in the local drug store offered help in emergencies. The telephone also opened a new avenue of employment for white women, that of the "hello girls" who worked as operators at the switchboards for the exchanges. Together, the telegraph and the telephone created the fast national and international network of communications that fed the metropolitan newspapers and downtown offices.

The automatic telegraph and the new telephone, although they added significantly to the reach of a business office, did not replace the need for personal, face-to-face dealing among businessmen, clerks, lawyers, accountants, brokers, and salesmen of all kinds. As the scale of corporate dealings expanded, so did the need for concentrations of office workers. As a result the office downtown rose upward.

Buildings ten to twenty stories tall replaced the former cast-iron rows of five to eight stories, and a few corporations built signature skyscrapers twenty to sixty stories tall. After 1895 the City's building code permitted steel frame construction and imposed no height limit. At the same time the new electric elevators allowed buildings to be constructed with elevator cores and sunlit offices around their edges. A normal office building laid out offices twenty feet in width from exterior window to interior wall so that sunlight could illuminate the desks. At the same time the inheritance of narrow streets from the earliest days and the attendant small parcels of land encouraged the building of tall, narrow buildings.

Although a few corporations built skyscrapers to advertise themselves, they rarely required more than a few floors for themselves. Instead, thousands of small companies, lawyers, brokers, and dealers of all kinds clamoring for central office space filled the new large buildings. A new machine accompanied all this office work, the typewriter. At first the province of male clerks, it soon became a specialty of female stenographers and clerks who staffed the City's offices.[4]

The concentration of so many office workers in the downtown and the addition of elevated, streetcar, and rail commuting all centering there vastly enlarged the retail possibilities of that location. Just uptown from the office core a "fashion row" of five- and six-story cast-iron-front stores offered a full range of clothing and household goods. Where formerly dry goods, furniture, jewelry, crockery, toys, and packaged foods had been sold in separate stores, now a few enterprising merchants had brought all these elements into a new institution, the department store. Together all the store windows, the new electric lights, and the cluster of theaters, vaudeville houses, hotels, restaurants, and bars made the nighttime center of the City a fantasy land whose luxury any City dweller could enjoy by strolling on the sidewalk. The mile of offices, stores, hotels, and theaters at the hub of the industrial metropolis constituted a palace garden of commerce.

Figure 5.4 Department store, 1895. The department store was the most significant symbol of downtown America in the late nineteenth century. Downtown had long since emptied of most residents, and buildings were now built exclusively for commercial use; department stores selling clothing, accessories, and home goods and furnishings were the largest of these buildings. Outside on the streets of downtown, telegraph, electrical, and telephone lines were strewn from poles in ever growing numbers.

A century of business expansion had displaced many old houses in the oldest neighborhoods adjacent to the downtown, leaving pockets of cut-up old houses and rear yards of sheds and shanties scattered at the business edge. Here the newest immigrants, the Syrians, Chinese, and Greeks, settled. The downtown required low-wage workers to stoke its furnaces and clean its buildings, to deliver its goods, and to manufacture the clothing, furniture, and furnishings that it sold in its stores. Jewish immigrants from Russia and the Austro-Hungarian Empire came in waves at the end of the nineteenth century fleeing persecution and poverty. They settled next the downtown at its northern retail edge.[5] Theirs was a comparatively new neighborhood of tenements, most of their buildings following a design that had been invented in 1878. This standard model had stores on the ground floor and four or five stories of apartments above, four apartments and a water closet per floor. The structure filled all but ten feet of a 25-by-100-foot lot, with a small indentation in one wall to make an air shaft that lit the stairwell.[6]

In the older, pre-1878 tenements, landlords provided only a cold-water tap on each floor and a toilet in the basement for every twenty residents. Enforcement of both sanitary and fire escape rules was lax. Together, old and new tenements created some of the densest human settlement of any world city. Poverty forced room overcrowding as poor immigrants took in relatives and boarders to help meet the rents. The stores and pushcarts filled the streets with shoppers, children, boxes, and mountains of trash. In fact conditions in the streets of crowded tenements were such that reformers were able to conduct a successful campaign to stop the construction of such land-crowding buildings.[7]

A subtle environmental change, however, had been in process for half a century, and now even the poorest neighborhoods attained a level of human habitability that they had lacked during the early nineteenth century. The drop in the price of food that continued after the 1873 depression allowed the poor to obtain something close to an adequate diet. Now, too, the abundance of clean water employed in washing food and the use of refrigeration to prevent spoilage reduced the frequency with which the poor consumed dangerous and spoiled foodstuffs. Finally, the discovery of germs and the subsequent drive for cleanliness made substantial inroads in infant mortality. Altogether these environmental changes allowed the resident population of the City, and of all modern cities with a population in excess of 50,000 inhabitants, to maintain itself by natural reproduction for the first time in human history.[8]

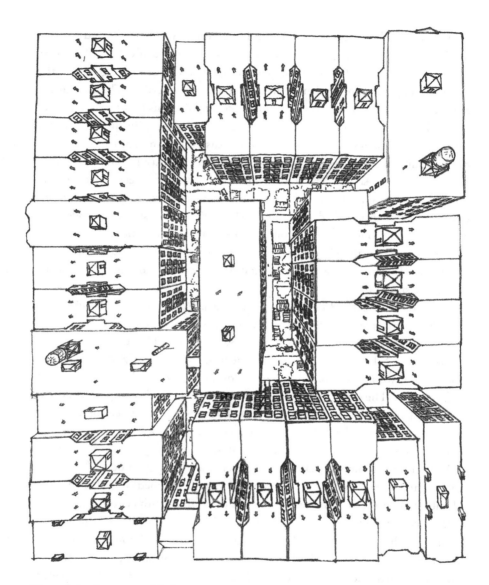

Figure 5.5   A tenement block, 1895. Immigrants of the late nineteenth century crowded into the four- to six-story tenements around the City's downtown. Before regulation that mandated air shafts, many rooms had been windowless. Even after, these "dumbbell tenements," so-called because of the shape they took to facilitate air shafts while abutting one another, were cramped, and their air shafts filled with trash in the absence of good public sanitary services. Each building had a privy, usually located in the small rear yard; each building also contained up to ten families and several individual boarders.

CHAPTER 5

Despite this significant improvement in mortality rates, the City's residents had to make their way within an economy that moved in cycles of boom and bust, a system that brought riches for some and suffering for many. The deep and long-lasting depression of 1873–1878 brought wages crashing down; they only recovered their former levels after twenty years. In 1877 railroad workers took up arms in a national strike that ultimately failed. It did, however, send ripples of fear of revolution and socialism through the minds of many.

Formidable obstacles of custom, business practice, and law confronted both union and political organizing. Waves of new immigrants filled a large pool of cheap surplus labor that employers could dip into at will. Union organizers had to cope with the conflicting loyalties of their fellows, concerns for family, and loyalties to the neighborhood. Factories staffed by sixteen- to twenty-year-old girls paid them less than a living wage because their earnings were regarded as family supplements, and besides they were expected to marry soon. Many did not. To the surprise of many, some of these women became stalwart union members.

These years showed the greatest income disparities until the early years of the twenty-first century, and the critics were many and loud. The list included the Knights of Labor, who wanted workers' committees on the shop floor to negotiate with their employers. A popular reform group led by Henry George (1839–1897) promoted the idea of a single tax based on land that would be adequate to support all branches of government. There were those who worked for municipal ownership of utilities, and the Populists who advocated currency and banking reform. Christian socialists imagined worker-controlled businesses, and Marxian socialists called for worker ownership of all the means of production. Finally, there were the various angry and frustrated workers who battled the police who were sent against them. It would take yet another half-century of business reform and much labor and political conflict before labor, business, and government could agree on the means to stabilize the nation's economy.

Although industrial unionism proved impossible as yet, a complex series of maneuvers that combined political action with craft and ethnic solidarity did allow an advance in craft unions. Unions had some success in the City by getting their members to refuse to purchase products offered by objectionable employers. The courts, however, determined that such boycotts amounted to a criminal interference in private business, and sentenced the leaders to four and five years in prison, a precedent only overturned by federal labor legislation in 1938. A union could even be subject to an injunction for ordering a strike. Also, in this era of rapid corporate consolidation, local firms became parts of large corporations that could afford to hire private police to break strikes. Owners found allies in local political bosses who wanted the favor of jobs for their constituents in exchange for their opposition to labor actions. The Catholic Church, which in the 1880s had had a sympathetic leadership that favored workers, now took a Romanized turn toward the European Church's fear of labor. It disowned the supportive priests and took a strong stand against labor ideas and labor politics. Instead, it urged its parishioners to follow the conservatism of the City's bishop and to shun unions, socialists, and anarchists.[9] In these years the Catholic Church and the ward machines were bastions of conservatism.

National origin strongly influenced labor relationships during this decade. "American workers," that is, skilled native-born Irish, German, and Yankee men who had mastered some difficult technique, were often able to establish customs for the shop that worked around and checked the power of the foreman. The German cigar makers agreed among themselves to stop working after ten hours and thereby won a much-coveted shortened day. Jewish immigrant garment workers, clustered in one warren of the City, noted the timing of seasonal orders of the buyers who came to the City to make their selections. By timing their strikes to occur at this strategic moment, they won 70 percent of their confrontations in the decade prior to 1895. Such successes brought a revival of the union movement in the late 1890s, with a surge of membership in craft union organizations like the American Federation of Labor. This group restricted its members to fellow craftsmen and operatives and sought wage and hour gains only. This movement did not, as others had formerly, organize whole factories or make demands for a new society.

STREETCAR SUBURBS

Beyond the downtown and districts of poverty, the application of electric power transformed the City's residential form. The electrification of the horsecar lines increased the speed of the streetcars to 12 miles per hour, and thereby allowed the lines to stretch out into green fields five to seven miles from the center of the City. The traction monopoly even opened an amusement park next the sea at the terminus of its eastern line. The development of the properties along the electrified lines followed a mix of old ways of building with new patterns of commercial and residential land use.

The main streets that served the electrified street railways offered the best retail locations, so that new residential areas were lined with retail strips: stores on the ground floor, apartments above. These neighborhood-serving stores sold meat and groceries on monthly credit accounts, thereby tiding their customers over short financial crises, but in deep depression storekeeper and customer could sink into bankruptcy together. From such a streetcar beginning, the suburban retail strip advanced to take its place as a universal element of American urban form.

Figure 5.6   Streetcar suburb, 1895. The arrival of the streetcar in the 1890s enabled a massive expansion of the City's footprint. Middle-class people moved to peripheral neighborhoods stretching out from the center on arterials on which streetcars ran. Builders lined these neighborhoods' streets with rows of two- to three-story townhouses and duplexes.

The mode of construction on the new fringe land continued old practices, but now successful subdivisions depended on gas, water, and sewer lines being laid in the new streets. This need for big city infrastructure persuaded many of the City's neighboring towns and villages to seek annexation to secure the City's utilities.

As in the past, speculating landowners cut up their fields and woods to offer lots for sale. Without supervision they designed streets for their properties so that they formed the maximum number of narrow lots whose fronts faced the street. A new municipal institution, the Board of Survey, exercised some slight control over subdividers. It limited its goals to making sure the new streets connected well to the old.

Carpenters and other craftsmen who built three to six houses a year took most of the lots for development; some families purchased a lot to build on their own account. Whether builder or homeowner, their financing rested on short-term, straight-line mortgages whose principal fell due in five to seven years. Many depended on paying a down payment and then no principal, hoping that the mortgage would be renewed at the end of its term. When depressions tightened the mortgage market, renewals ceased and uncounted numbers of mortgagors lost their properties.

In a city-building process of many small entrepreneurs, little innovation could be expected. Everyone sought market safety in repeating what was known and proven popular. Thus, without legal regulations, custom and fear of failure directed the design of the vast new areas of streetcar suburbs.

In the City's new areas the row house fashion continued, and land abundance allowed the lots to grow a little. There was now room for a front porch and a rear yard where, in addition to the housewife's laundry lines, a small garden and a fruit tree or grape arbor could be planted. Inside the house, cast-iron coal stoves proved a popular new appliance, and they fostered a broad fashion in home baking. In all but the most minimal new houses, steam heat and a full bath added to everyone's comfort.

Freestanding wooden, stone, and brick houses characterized the new neighborhoods of the well-to-do. Often here the subdividers added covenants against the building of livery stables, saloons, or manufacturing and set requirements for lot lines and the control of fences. These private arrangements would become the models for zoning laws twenty-five years later. They continue to be elaborated today in twentieth- and twenty-first-century homeowner association rules. The covenants of the late nineteenth and early twentieth centuries also took on an antisocial dimension. They often forbade the sale of such properties to Jews and African Americans. It was not until 1948 that such restrictions were ruled unenforceable.

By such a process that mixed old building ways with new infrastructure and new amenities, the modern class-graded residential suburb emerged. Because only the well-to-do could afford freestanding single-family houses on good-sized lots, such neighborhoods achieved a degree of exclusivity. The next social filter came with the distinction between those who could afford any kind of new construction and those who could not. The final cut divided those who rented in older structures, but who could afford to commute to work, from those for whom the streetcar ride was too costly or too inconvenient. For those who must walk, the old City remained their home.

An Immigrants' City

Boatloads of southern Italians, eastern European Jews, and residents of the Austro-Hungarian Empire arrived during the 1880s and 1890s, and Chinese workmen from California joined these newcomers. The children and grandchildren of these latecomers were able in time to participate in the nation's twentieth-century prosperity.

Class grading had always existed in the City, but now in the City of 1895 a new pattern of class and ethnic segregation prevailed. Immigrants coming from the same areas settled together. No one group occupied every room in every building over an entire block, but the concentrations of fellows and the gathering of supporting stores, churches, and synagogues brought forth the Little Italy, Chinatown, Little England, Jewish Ghetto, and Klein Deutschland for which the 1890s are famous.[10]

Invidious comparisons, stereotypes, and hostile nicknames pervaded the City as immigration forced residents to deal with foreign languages and strangers. Nevertheless, the American civic melting pot continued to function. By 1895 a fresh definition of "American" emerged, meaning native-born whites of Irish, German, or old-stock parents. This crude inclusiveness embraced the large residential areas of the City where children of former immigrants and natives lived side by side. It had not been an easy transition from the nativist pre-Civil War City of Protestants, but a rough harmony prevailed despite a very active parochial school-building program of the Catholic bishops that fanned Protestant prejudice. The class-filtering effects of the housing market encouraged residential toleration among these groups. Public school or parochial school, your neighbor was roughly like yourself.

Alone among all the groups of the poor, the City denied African Americans their hopes for prosperity. Contemporary white prejudice erected a long-lasting barrier forbidding their entry into industrial employments. African Americans were Americans through and through, as long resident on this continent as any Puritan descendant. They spoke English, 80–90 percent of them could read and write; they were as ready for industrial employment as any group, but they could not be hired to work in the new industrial economy.[11]

The deep traditions of American prejudice had taken on an added layer at the end of the century. A new cultural fashion celebrated the rich and the powerful by twisting Darwin's evolutionary theory to propose the genetic inferiority of nonwhites. Such a self-satisfying version of science ignored the examples at hand in the City: the upstanding African American doctors, lawyers, coal merchants, caterers, lumber dealers, and the few artisans who had found a corner in the skilled trades. As a consequence, for most, to be an African American in the City meant enduring a life of poverty. Their employments remained the old ones of laborer, domestic, waiter, hod carrier, stevedore, teamster, and barber.

Prejudice in turn relegated the City's 80,000 African Americans to a special place in the local economy. White politicians and police found it advantageous to confine illegal businesses to African American neighborhoods. Here brothels and gambling joints could front as political clubs, and local voters could be organized for a little cash to vote as told. In such a setting the City's white law could not provide justice in disputes; violence ruled.

This absence of civil order and justice in the African American community brought enduring consequences in its wake. All white groups had criminal gangs, especially in the years of a group's first entrance to the City. In time municipal and state authorities brought their gangs under some control, but the criminal rule persisted in many black communities by white connivance in illegal activities. This old practice visited an enduring curse of gangs and their violence upon African American communities.[12]

A position of respectable citizenship proved ever elusive. During the last decades of the nineteenth century some new musical avenues offered slight progress. Gospel singing groups from the new African American colleges in the

South toured the North. Showmen mounted very polished and ambitious programs with choruses of one hundred singers. The popular African American dance, the cakewalk, caught the attention of society hostesses who sought instruction for their guests. In all these roles, the African American remained the servant and the entertainer, but this path opened outward a few years later to the role of admired and respected jazz musician and composer. Music thereby pried open a hole in the City's fence of intense prejudice.[13]

By means of self-selection and income grading, the City's neighborhoods settled into a quiescent pattern that reduced the likelihood of a reappearance of the riots of midcentury or the violent railroad strikes of 1877. There were, to be sure, times when accumulated angers and frustrations burst into sudden strikes and rock throwing at the police. Often such outbursts went forward against the advice of union leaders who were trying to establish regular bargaining practices with employers, but even an occasional citywide strike of streetcar operators did not disrupt the city.

The concentrations of new immigrants transformed local politics by requiring that local leaders alter their appeals and services to reflect the attitudes and needs of surrounding neighbors. A long-enduring ward boss might find his home turf changing from working-class native-born Yankees or Irish to immigrant Jews or Italians. Each group needed jobs, and help in bargaining with the law. Fortunately for the bosses, contemporary additions to the infrastructure— streets, wires, pipes, and parks—afforded jobs to parcel out.

The shift to organized ward and precinct politics established a pattern that endured in municipal government for many years. The local political bosses decided who would fill the seats in the City Council, but they found it necessary to make agreements with business leaders concerning candidates for mayor. As a result, merchants and lawyers continued to govern from the mayor's office, but their economizing propensities had to be tempered with attention to jobs for ward constituents.

The wealthy remained active as cultural leaders even as their electoral influence weakened. Their large houses, carriages, parties, weddings, and women's dresses set the fashions of the day. For the many to whom all this was denied, the metropolitan Sunday newspapers reported in detail on the doings of the local rich. The former fashion of large row houses in the near east side of the City shifted to a few nearby north-running, tree-lined streets graced with freestanding mansions. Beyond the city the gentleman's custom of the country estate continued, but the railroad brought it new neighbors in the form of villages of wealthy downtown commuters who raised large homes near the stations.

Some of the new cultural patterns of the rich became transformed in time to be enduring institutions in the City. The wealthy now studied in American universities and abroad. Their enthusiasm for large libraries in their homes extended to support for public libraries to replace the existing private athenaeums founded years earlier.

The wealthy traveled to Europe to hear concerts and operas and to visit collections of the fine arts. At home these experiences translated into a symphony orchestra and hall, an opera company and opera house, and a fine arts museum. To the rich, the City offered a valued audience to play before. In each new institution, they took the role of donors, trustees, and managers while the public attended according to its own cultural traditions—many coming for books to read, some for symphonies, others for operas and museums.

An ominous trend also set in among the rich during these years. The local elite shut themselves up in clubs that no longer represented the spectrum of the City's successful. Elite prejudice against Jews had so increased since the Civil War that clubmen denied membership to the son of a founder of the Union League Club.[14] The children of the rich no longer attended the City's public schools, but were sent for training to fashionable New England preparatory schools and thence to colleges that restricted their clientele. In these years of the 1890s, the strongly Protestant, anti-Semitic, anti-African American elite began to form into a national corps. Their self-isolation boded poorly for a future when the rich and powerful of the nation would be ignorant of its cities and its citizens.

6

Toward a New Economy and a Novel Urban Form, 1925

Figure 6.1   The City as it appeared in 1920.

During the previous thirty years the metropolitan region had doubled in population. Within the City's municipal boundaries the number of residents increased by 70 percent, but the suburban population multiplied by two and a half times, so that in 1925 the City contained 2,000,000, the suburbs 500,000.

The origins of the newcomers changed yet one more time, from overseas immigrants to American rural migrants, black and white. Beginning in 1921, farm prices in the United States collapsed, ushering in a twenty-year farm depression. As a result, many country people, white and African American, moved to the City to better their fortunes. Meanwhile a national political campaign also forced a change in the composition of newcomers. Nativism had revived following the 1880s shift in the immigrant pool from Germany and the United Kingdom to eastern and southern Europe. The commonplace distrust and fear of strangers had taken on a spurious scientific rationale that claimed an innate superiority for northern Europeans and educated white Anglo-Saxons and denigrated others, both white and black. The Russian Communist revolution of 1917 and the German and Hungarian revolutions of 1919 sparked a "Red Scare" in the United States that branded immigrant labor leaders as revolutionary socialists, and many eastern Europeans as dangerous radicals. All three sentiments merged to support the passage of the 1921 and 1924 immigration laws that, in time, limited the admission of eastern and southern Europeans to the United States. In such a climate of postwar opinion, industrialists and businessmen used the popular fears and prejudices to crush labor unions. Labor in the City retreated into its old craft union form, and even the associations of skilled workers lost members.

The economic base for the City's growth and prosperity during the twenties combined old and new elements. The long-standing seafaring function had been renewed by the construction of new transatlantic docks on the south side of the harbor. The large pool of young workers, foreign and native-born, continued to support the City's machine-tending enterprises: an enormous range of processes from pressing on typewriter and adding machine keys to sewing, box making, and steel fabrication. The City during the twenties remained a manufacturing city.

A new economy of marketing and finance undergirded the City of 1925. Its institutions fostered contradictory expansion paths, supporting both the downtown central stores and skyscrapers and the suburban expansion based on the automobile.

After World War I, new intermediary agents gathered next the downtown: public relations offices and advertising promoters and brokers to facilitate the seller's courtship of the retail customer. The public relations men made up stories for the newspapers to make their clients seem exciting and newsworthy. They gave an aura of glamour to the latest-model cars, the radio and film actors and actresses, the changes in seasonal clothing. At the same time the advertising offices blanketed the City's monthly magazines, public spaces, newspapers, and radio networks with text and pictures calculated to connect the client's product to common human desires—beauty, health, power, wealth, status, sexual attractiveness. The soap was pure, the cereal would make you strong, beautiful women admired the car.

A sustained big budget for advertising allowed the manufacturers of branded products to compete among themselves without the necessity of cutting prices when demand slackened. The big firms respected each other's prices and competed over styles and promotions. Already by 1894 Coca-Cola was spending one million dollars to advertise its five-cent product.[1] More and more firms followed these early precedents, and the City's downtown soon sprouted the offices of these marketers.

A new line of products and new modes of finance accompanied this merchandising shift. In the postwar boom, consumers could afford to purchase a much wider range of products than formerly when food, clothing, and rent ate up most of a family's budget. Expensive consumer durables grabbed their attention: radios, phonographs, player pianos, mechanical refrigerators, vacuum cleaners, washing machines, and automobiles. Few Americans, however, had sufficient savings to purchase these items outright; they needed credit.

Before the war, automobiles had been a luxury item, sold to the rich for cash, but in 1919 General Motors sought a new market by establishing its own lending corporation. Personal finance corporations came forward to advance money on the basis of a borrower's paycheck. John Wanamaker issued charge plates to his customers, so that credit would flow at the instant of purchase in his department store. From 1922 through 1929 three-quarters of the automobiles and consumer durables were sold on time contracts. The salesperson gave you the goods for free; you promised to pay in the future.[2] It was thus that these first decades of the twentieth century launched what we now call the consumer economy.

Time sales proved a boon to downtown stores, but events both within and outside the downtown brought the whole system crashing down at the close of the decade. Speculation in real estate would throw up a paper edifice that could not be sustained.

THE SHAPE OF THE METROPOLIS

By 1925 the centralizing tendencies of the past century had resulted in the dense urban form that we look back upon today as the apogee of the American city. A metropolitan pattern of hub and spokes placed the office skyscrapers, department stores, theaters, luxury apartment towers, factory and warehouse districts, and residential neighborhoods within the geography and rhythms of the railroad, the subway, and the streetcar.

Four major events reshaped the form of the City during this decade: the closing of southern and eastern European immigration, the massive increase in automobile ownership, the enactment of land use controls and zoning, and financial innovations in consumer and real estate lending. Together these new events began a process of transforming the highly concentrated City into a multicentered racially and class-patterned form of the later low-density metropolis.

This City hosted an ever-growing concentration of financial capital. Equipped with its new bureaucratic corporate forms, the City's banks, insurance companies, and investment houses fostered new lines of business: electric power generation, the electrification of homes and businesses, the elaboration of the chemical and petroleum industries, the manufacture and marketing of automobiles, and the communication cluster of telephones, radio, and film. These capital investments fostered two contradictory tendencies in the shape of the City. A variety of additions both intensified its centralizing habits and stretched its streetcar suburbs outward with the addition of the paved street and the private automobile. Indeed, the automobile encouraged new residential construction closer in, in the neglected spaces between the outward-fanning lines of the railroad and the streetcar.

The increase in centralization stemmed in part from two new bridges and a subway connecting to an existing elevated that joined the downtown to the across-the-harbor industrial satellite of the City. Private subway companies added new lines to link the downtown to outlying industrial, residential, and

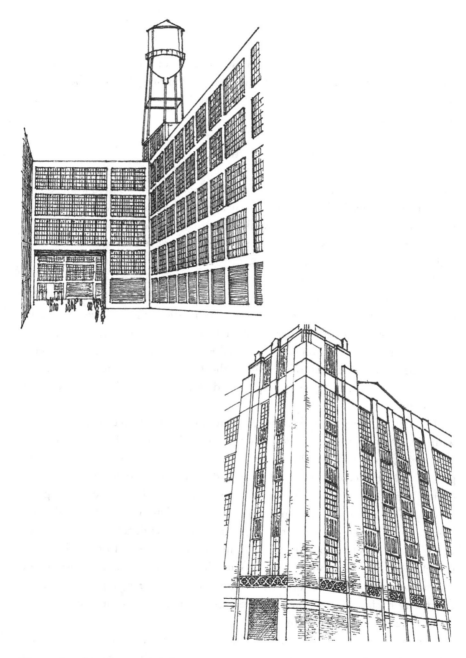

Figures 6.2, 6.3 An automobile plant, 1925. The modern factory was of steel frame and reinforced-concrete construction, enabling a large amount of space for windows and for assembly-line manufacturing; the interior court was very utilitarian in appearance. The exterior, however, was still given a masonry skin that gave it the look of a more classical structure.

CHAPTER 6

entertainment districts. Many areas of the City, however, remained outside these transit investments because subway enlargement proposals met strong opposition from subcenters that decried the heavy costs of new subway construction.

The former merchant quarter and later downtown now sprang up in yet another new form: the tower town. The eight- to twelve-story office buildings of previous decades now pushed upward to become skyscrapers of fifteen and twenty stories. A City height limit was removed in 1920 and developers'

Figure 6.4 Amusement park, 1925. On the shore of the bay, at the terminus of several transit lines, a privately run recreational park thrived from after the Civil War until the 1950s. At first it was modest, consisting of groomed beaches and bathhouses. By the 1920s, however, it featured a boardwalk, numerous commercial stalls, a Ferris wheel, and a rollercoaster. With suburbanization and the availability of home entertainment, the park's popularity declined, and it eventually closed in the 1960s.

enthusiasm pushed buildings even higher from then on, though these skyscrapers were still subject to setbacks at higher stories for the purpose of allowing daylight into city streets.

The skyscrapers of the teens and twenties rose out of the extreme concentration of businesses and business services at one central place. Here in the downtown gathered national and international networks of telephone, telegraph, and cable services, the major private banks and the regional branch of the Federal Reserve, as well as corporate offices of railroads and other large depositors. The business advantages of working in this concentrated hive drove up office rents to such a degree that twenty-, thirty-, and forty-story office towers became a successful investment. Although some of the skyscrapers took the names of the corporations that financed their construction, the Woolworth Building, Metropolitan Life Insurance Building, United Shoe Machinery Building, and the like, the skyscraper of the twenties did not furnish all its floors for the corporate sponsor. Instead the towers held hundreds of small tenants, most leasing 800 to 1,000 square feet to house eight or ten employees. Lawyers, accountants, small firms and brokers of all kinds made the financial district skyscrapers the home of small-scale capitalists that together serviced the financial markets.

The private railroad corporations now consolidated into two regional lines, and together they constructed a giant neoclassical union station in the old slum areas on the western edge of the downtown. To the east, luxury apartments surrounded an eighteenth-century park. The apartments' location near the old eastern commuter rail station made them geographic anchors of a corridor of wealth and luxury that stretched north from the City to suburbs six and ten miles away. Along this way, a line of automobile showrooms formed a retail parade designed to lure the well-to-do to this new product.

The City's center now boasted something quite new: the blending, in one continuous stretched-out area, of the financial center, the shopper's downtown, the entertainment downtown, the hotel visitor's downtown, and the opera and symphony concert downtown. The popularity of this new place, its crowds, heaps of goods, and glow of lights, foretold a new economy that would in time replace the industrial-based City. Half a dozen and more blocks north of the office towers, a cluster of department stores and retail specialty shops, theaters and hotels together formed a place of fashion and entertainment, a gathering of marketing designed to mobilize the populace's wishes and fantasies. Never before had such a fusion of merchandise and theatricality come together. In the past the cluster of merchant houses, a city hall, or a market had served as town centers. Now from all over the metropolis visitors sought the City's novel and varied downtown.

To maintain some order within this mixed area, to prevent multistory manufacturing from encroaching on streets of fashion, and to prevent massive office buildings from overwhelming their neighbors, the City adopted a new and powerful set of regulations: zoning laws, and it established a Planning Board to lay out the zones.[3] The zoning ordinance specified the height limits and upper-story setbacks, and it separated economic functions by allocating very large areas exclusively to residential, commercial, or industrial uses. Next to the harbor and along the railroad corridors the zoning map designated wide swaths of land for possible industrial expansion. The downtown and the main streets of the City and the old village gathering of stores the ordinance rewarded with wide swaths for commercial development.

In addition to the support from downtown real estate interests, residential developers pressed for zoning because they wanted to promote property values, especially in the new areas of single-family houses. They could ensure uniformity in parcels they owned by means of covenants, but they could not control neighboring land they did not own. Therefore they demanded zoning laws that would establish broad areas for similar housing types, encouraging large-scale speculative building.[4]

The zoning task required some years of research to gather all the details of the City's buildings and land uses, and to prepare a legally enforceable map indicating the boundaries of each zone. Thereafter the ubiquity of zoned land imposed upon every major real estate undertaking the need to make its way through the public process of the Planning and Zoning Boards. In the past, the development of urban land had often involved some political maneuvers; but now, from the zoned twenties onward, real estate truly became a matter of municipal politics.

Meanwhile, wartime employment and the postwar boom enabled a considerable number of immigrant families to find newer and easier quarters in the nearby suburbs of the City. At the same time the enforcement of the City's newly enacted building and health codes for multiunit housing forced landlords to undertake at least a few basic safety measures. New regulations forbade the time-honored custom of cutting up old houses into windowless cells. Fire

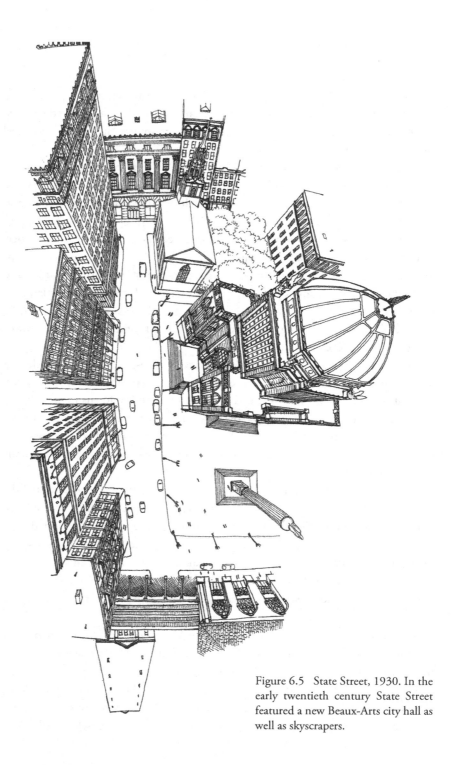

Figure 6.5   State Street, 1930. In the early twentieth century State Street featured a new Beaux-Arts city hall as well as skyscrapers.

escapes sprouted from multiple-story tenements, and at least running water, a sink, and a toilet commonly appeared on each floor. Rather than incur these expenses, some landlords closed off their upper stories and leased only the retail ground floor. During the twenties, bit by bit, the City's most crowded wards saw their densities fall. Room overcrowding lessened and sanitary conditions improved.

Beyond the City's center, the decade launched new patterns of urban growth by means of road construction, subdivision planning, and commercial finance. During the postwar years the City spent huge sums on widening and paving streets, even introducing such now-commonplace details as traffic signals. In the retail downtown it widened the main avenue in 1912, and throughout the City it sought to relieve traffic congestion by establishing, where possible, uniform widths for the main arteries. The ever-increasing sales of automobiles defeated these efforts, however, so that the City's street engineers were forced to learn what highway engineers later forgot: an improved street attracts more traffic. The City also undertook to pave the main streets that led to new residential areas. Along these arteries, now crowded with streetcars and automobiles, stores lined the sidewalks and former village centers thickened up as subcenters for local shopping. The new federal intercity highways, the U.S. Routes, begun in 1916, enlarged upon the retail strip patterns of the streetcar. Now the U.S. Routes sprouted a forest of signs, gas stations, services, and roadside shops seeking to catch the motorists' business.

The prosperity of the decade fired a real estate boom. At the outset, in 1920, 80 percent of the City's housing units were rentals, and, since apartment living had now become a familiar pattern for families, apartment house construction accelerated. A few downtown apartments took the form of luxury towers, but most were four-story, steam-heated, elevator apartment houses. Apartment developers sought the main streets where an old house could be torn down or a vacant lot would take a few units. The former village centers of the close-in suburbs were the most popular locations for such construction.

In the consumer climate of the twenties, land speculators promoted the possibility of home ownership. Indeed, the City's proportion of homeowners rose to 27 percent after a decade.[5] The majority of these houses went up in the suburban areas of the metropolis, land six to ten miles from the downtown. Zoning now guided the building process by separating single-family and two-family houses from apartment buildings and stores, but zoning did not alter the character of the subdivision of land or the old bit-by-bit process of house building. The familiar sequence began with the speculator purchasing some farm fields, preparing a few unpaved streets, and slicing his blocks into small 4,000- to 7,000-square-foot lots. These he sold either to small builders or to individuals who arranged for the construction of their own houses. He also sold lots to small investors by promising them that resales would soon bring them handsome profits. The speculator's hope was to sell off his lots in a year and to move out a bit farther to purchase a little more land. For the past 250 years the City had been built in this way, and to this process may be attributed the pre-1950s common jumble of architectural styles and lot arrangements.

Figure 6.6 Dutch colonial house, 1920. The Dutch colonial, with its gambrel roof, was a standard of early twentieth-century suburbia in the Northeast.

CHAPTER 6

At the high end of the market, however, a new and influential method of land preparation and sales had begun. A few speculators, supplied with generous bank credit, purchased large tracts of land, laid out streets and lots for single-family houses for the wealthy, and maintained a uniformity of landscaping and building placement by the use of covenants. These subdivisions commonly arranged themselves around a golf club, and a few developed shopping centers as well.

These large-scale "community builders" popularized the designs that subsequently became the standards adopted by the federal government and planning boards everywhere. The list is impressive: a careful ordering of arterial and interior streets, the lesser streets making up the interior circulation; superblocks and cul-de-sacs; planting strips between curb and sidewalk; setback lines and lot coverage restrictions; planned placement of parks and playgrounds; and provision for utility easements. By the advent of World War II these design elements became the everyday methods used in middle-income suburban development.[6]

Like the phonograph, piano, and automobile, the real estate boom rested on time purchase, in this case on first and second mortgages. Since the 1890s the practice of mortgage lending had shifted to a considerable degree toward institutions and away from individual lenders. Private local investors had always dominated the business because they were in a position to visit the property in question and to make an informed estimate of its value. Savings banks, commercial banks, savings and loan associations, and insurance companies ignored this detailed examination at their peril. Since so much depended on these local evaluations, during the twenties no national market in mortgages yet existed, but one novelty flourished briefly.

Bond houses entered the commercial real estate finance market. Beginning in the nineties bond houses offered 100 percent financing for the construction of commercial buildings at an interest rate 2–4 percent above market levels. After making its loan to the developer, the bond house issued bonds against these properties in small denominations to retail customers. At one point during the twenties one billion dollars in such debentures stood outstanding. When the real estate market collapsed in 1930, the bond houses declared bankruptcy and their bonds fell into default.[7]

The common deal for apartment houses and commercial properties asked the developers to put up 20 percent of the cost of the project. The banks or insurance companies then lent 50 percent on a first mortgage and 20–30 percent more on a second mortgage. The first mortgages commonly ran for ten years with interest paid semiannually, and the principal fell due at the end of the term. Most developers hoped to sell their properties and to let the purchaser assume the loans. The purchaser in turn expected that the first mortgage would be renewed and that the rents would allow the second mortgage to be quickly extinguished. Second mortgages ran for five to seven years and their interest ranged up from 12 percent.

Home mortgages followed a pattern similar to commercial loans. All but some amortizing mortgages were short-term, five to seven years. Many second mortgages on homes adopted the savings and loan association's amortizing mortgage. With this instrument the borrower paid the interest and some fraction of the principal every month, paying it down little by little. Amortizing mortgages commonly ran eleven years.[8] Straight term or amortizing, all this mortgage debt rested upon the market prices of real property since 70–80 percent of the estimated value had been extended. In boom times, the inevitable tendency was to inflate estimates, so that as expectations rose the value of the loans came to exceed the sales price of the properties. Just such an event occurred in 1930.[9]

Farm prices had collapsed in 1921 and the nation's enormous farm population fell steadily into debt and failure. Urban retail sales reached their peak in 1926, but both these signals were ignored by the real estate and stock markets, until both collapsed. Laden with worthless mortgages, 4,800 banks failed. A number of these had been established as elements within suburban speculation schemes. The subsequent economic depression forced 20 percent of the region's workers into unemployment, and years of widespread suffering ensued. The City's initiation of the consumer economy came to a harsh conclusion in 1930. Its private elements, retail credit and short-term mortgages, could not function successfully without governmental regulations to control speculation and without continuous federal adjustments to the national money markets.

THE MELTING POT

Within the City's old neighborhoods and the near suburbs, immigrants and their children shouldered the task of forming some kind of ethnic identity while at the same time joining the universal culture that Americans demanded.

Churches, synagogues, temples, parochial schools, fraternal organizations, and hyphenated organizations of all kinds multiplied as immigrants and their children fashioned the ever-changing cultural mix that in the United States combines the "rainbow" with the "melting pot."

The expansion of industrial and service employment during the first decades of the twentieth century drew to the City a massive migration of African Americans from the South Atlantic states and the West Indies. A perceptive observer called the new arrivals "peasants with a railroad ticket and a suitcase," thereby likening them to their European counterparts.[10] The women continued to concentrate in domestic employment, and the men still faced strong barriers to many industrial jobs. Some worked in labor gangs for the railroads, while the Pullman cars provided a new service niche for others.

Though these were prosperous times for many, lynchings continued unabated in the South and race riots broke out everywhere, including northern cities.[11] The scandal of rioting in the Illinois capital mobilized white settlement house workers and philanthropists to establish a political defense organization, the National Association for the Advancement of Colored People. In 1920, when James Weldon Johnson, a Florida migrant, became its director, the organization began to move toward more African American control. In 1910, a year after the NAACP had been founded, the Urban League was formed to help the migrants get settled and to find industrial jobs for them.

Within the City strong white hostility intensified the segregation of African Americans, newcomers and old residents alike, so that an all-black district began along the west side of the inner-city railroad tracks. Here, in a neighborhood that had first been Irish and then Jewish, the newcomers took over apartments on the main streets and small row houses on the blocks within. In this new center the contemporary international vogue of the "Negro" found American expression. The advance of African American music from cakewalk to ragtime and jazz broke through racial barriers, so that American popular music became a blend of the works of African American composers and their white Tin Pan Alley counterparts. Thanks to phonograph records and the radio, the music that emanated from the City soon found a national audience.[12]

The enactment of Prohibition in January 1920 intensified the earlier custom of whites visiting African American neighborhoods for illegal entertainments. Nightclubs featuring African American music and dance fashions, most notably the Charleston, stride piano, and jazz, attracted large nightly clienteles. Such were the customs of the time, however, that in these cabarets Jim Crow prevailed and African American customers were seated apart from the whites. In 1933, with the end of Prohibition, white patronage of the African American nightclubs faded.

Because the City was one of the nation's centers of magazine and book publishing, theater, broadcasting, and film, it drew to itself a pool of highly educated African Americans who had studied both in the South and the North and in Europe. Thus, writers and artists, actors and filmmakers joined the musicians in their ghetto. The collective works of all these newcomers came to be known as a "Renaissance." All these writers and artists embraced the latest modern forms and techniques in their goal of fashioning a culture that would supersede the earlier African American respectability that whites had spurned. Pride and assertion formed their common voice. African American concerns were not those of the white "lost generation" who struggled with the moral bankruptcy of World War I.

The Renaissance writers and artists hoped that by political assertion they could demonstrate the validity of their culture, first to appeal to the large and ever more literate African American audience, but also to catch the attention of some influential whites. Theirs had been a unique experience for three hundred years; wanting to fashion a separate culture and impatient with white rejection and segregation, they sought an alternative to the melting pot.

A special feature of these Renaissance writers and artists lay in their embrace of "low-down folks," their ghetto neighbors and the newcomers from the small towns of the Atlantic South. With their own novels and modern poetry they also published books of traditional spirituals. African American literature and art continued to develop with energy and success long after the twenties. Historians looking back on these beginnings credit the practical interests of the "low-down," whose needs focused on the everyday issues of jobs and respect, for driving the elite forward into the Civil Rights era.

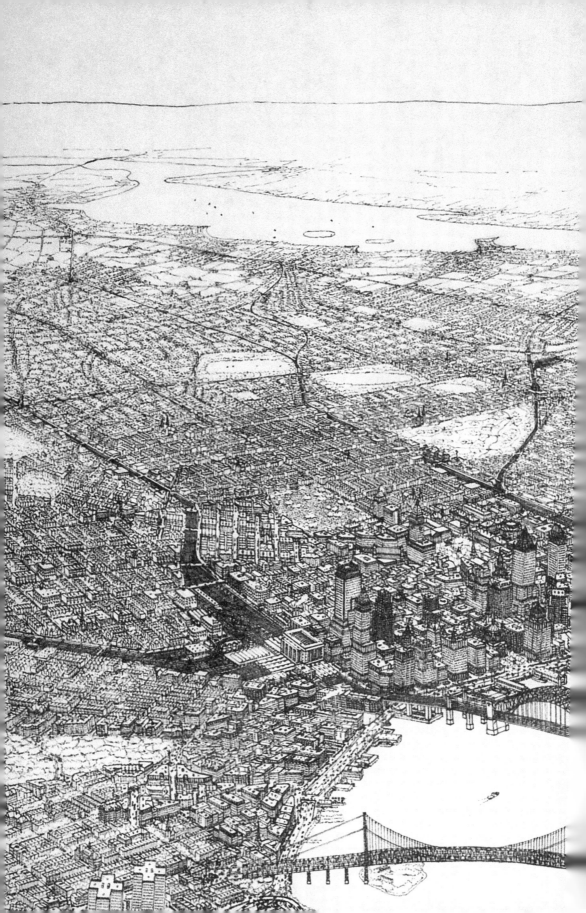

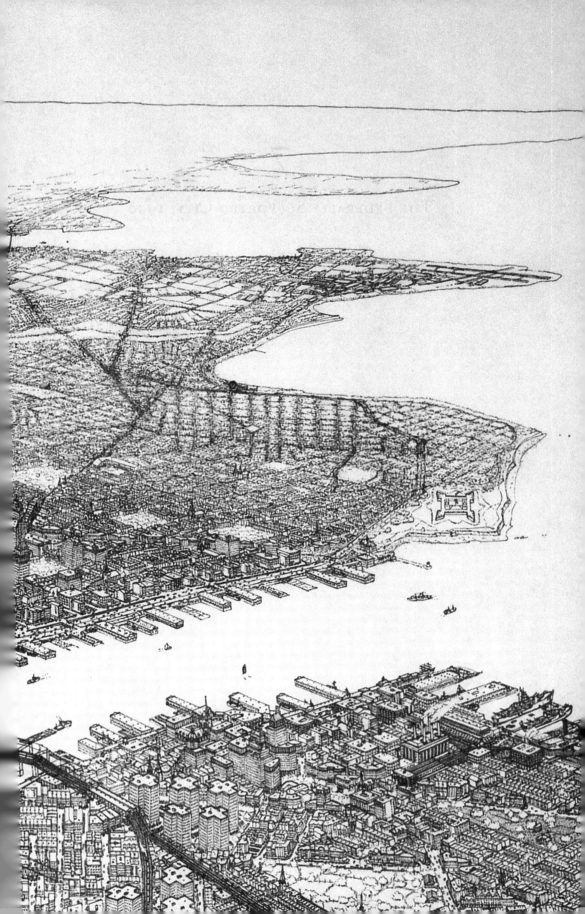

7

THE FEDERALLY SUPPORTED CITY, 1950

Figure 7.1 The City as it appeared in 1950.

The foundations for a new postwar city form grew out of a novel mixture of optimism and fear. After a decade of economic depression U.S. factories hummed to meet war demand, then postwar demand for goods and orders for overseas aid. Unlike those of Europe, Russia, China, and Japan, American cities had remained untouched by war's bombs and armies. The City's population once again swelled with the influx of factory labor. During the war the CIO and other unions fulfilled a no-strike pledge, and in return the government negotiated union-business contracts to avoid crippling strikes. After the war business and unions continued the wartime practice of giving benefit packages as part of collective bargaining, promoting widespread prosperity.

The port's small naval facility expanded and overtook much of the underutilized waterfront on the south side of the river. Americans were anxious to build anew, to enjoy the abundance of their industries, to try new ways, and to start a new generation of well-fed, well-clothed, well-housed, and well-educated children.

Yet war did not end. The Soviet Union set up puppet regimes in all the eastern European nations it had conquered from Germany. In China a Communist movement and army drove the old nationalist regime to the island of Formosa. In response, the U.S. government once again sponsored a postwar campaign of fear as it had in 1918 in response to the Russian Revolution. President Truman initiated a policy of supporting the American containment of Communism wherever it might appear, to prevent it from spreading beyond its 1949 boundaries. An atomic armaments race ensued. The United States exploded a hydrogen bomb in 1952; Russia followed in 1953. Ever since these years the City has lived under the fear of destruction by atomic attack. From 1950 to 1953 the nation fought yet another war to prevent the North Korean Communists from conquering the entire Korean Peninsula. At the same time it refused to stop the French reconquest of its former colony, Vietnam, thereby reversing the centuries-old United States tradition of favoring self-determination of national groups over their imperial masters.

In retrospect, two aspects of the fear of Communism appear to have played directly upon the fate of the City. First, the expenditures on war, armaments, and foreign economic and military aid, $35 billion from 1946 to 1952, had a Keynesian effect: the national government's purchases and spending kept up full employment in the United States. Second, the fear of Communism led to breaking up Communist-controlled labor unions and blacklisting radicals of all sorts. Thus the Red Scare shut down the communitarian and cooperative ideas and experiments of the New Deal years and lent political power to an emphasis on individual economic mobility over the equalitarian rights of citizenship.

The Form of the Postwar City

Despite a general climate of fear and conservatism after the war, the experience of the New Deal and the world war sustained a bipartisan sense that the federal government could and should accomplish major undertakings. In keeping with this optimistic mood, the U.S. Bureau of Roads, President Eisenhower, and a coalition of urban businessmen worked to further disperse the built landscape. While suburban growth had outpaced growth in the City since the 1920s, urban development after the Second World War represented a radical break defined by the nearly complete monopolization of growth by the suburbs, in large part due to government policies.

Underlying this revolution in urban form stood the automobile. In 1930 there was one car for every five persons in the region, and by 1950 the ratio had changed to one for every four.[1] During the Depression a new state authority using New Deal dollars built a modest network of four-lane roadways around the City. These were placed in the suburbs where they were integrated with the regional network of U.S. Routes. Some of these new roads took the form of planted and landscaped parkways abutting recreation areas. They featured grade-separated intersections: the crossing routes passed over or under the parkways with on- and off-ramps for access. These designs allowed traffic to flow on and off the parkways without stopping.

During the 1940s the City pursued a strategy of linking these suburban parkways to the City with a series of urban, waterfront highways. The City's downtown real estate owners hoped that these would ease traffic jams on the City's streets and allow more customers to come into the downtown to shop. In 1944 the Federal-Aid Highway Act allowed the use of federal funds for land acquisition in urban areas, so that by 1949 a quarter of the federal highway budget was devoted to urban highways. Unfortunately from the point of view of the center City's real estate owners, urban expressways hastened the decentralization of the City's metropolitan region and led to the loss of the office-store-theater downtown's regional dominance.[2]

Figure 7.2   Depression-era parkway. Depression-era funding allowed great infrastructure improvements in the area. Graded parkways for horses were improved for the automobile with asphalt, and a few states experimented with a new kind of limited-access highway with grade-separated intersections. Some of these, such as the one pictured here, were adorned with architecturally detailed bridges and planted medians.

Figure 7.3   Commercial strip, 1950. The growing use of the automobile had great implications for the commercial landscape. Commercial strips were now set back from the street by parking areas. Signage and many of the actual establishments were large and flamboyant, to allow drivers to easily recognize them at high speeds.

The City's suburbs gained 400,000 in the 1930s and 1940s, mostly middle- and upper-income residents from the city proper. The metropolitan population as a whole grew meagerly compared to past eras, to 2.9 million in 1950. Because this growth was largely automobile-driven, some of the main arterial streets and U.S. highways leading out of the city sprouted a new form of retail strip, with parking spaces and flamboyant signs and buildings located in front of the stores.

Manufacturing led the decentralization, but its abandonment of central locations did not cause the downtown to fail during the fifties. New industrial machine and assembly processes demanded more floor space than could be found in the old multistory factories of the City.[3] The norm for modern manufacture grew to be a one-story suburban building. Between the end of World War II and the mid-fifties the City lost 4 percent of its manufacturing jobs while its suburban counterparts added 30 percent to their total.[4] The City's suburbs became centers for the burgeoning aerospace, aviation, computer, and medical supply industries.

The downtown added a modest number of white-collar jobs in finance, insurance, real estate, publishing, and advertising. A few high-profile downtown real estate ventures had gone ahead in the 1930s, built in the Art Deco version of classicism that disguised structural elements in a flat relief style. After the war banks and insurance companies added a few more towers in the more stripped-down modern style.

Overall the downtown changed little. The movie palaces still filled. Department stores remained busy and the crowds still streamed in at Christmas. Downtown retailers, however, began to chase after their customers in the growing suburbs. Malls and big box retailing had yet to appear, but suburban branches of downtown stores, located in well-to-do established railroad suburbs, attracted more and more customers.

It was in these early postwar years that the focus of municipal effort shifted toward support of federal financial initiatives and away from its former concentration on public works for water, sewer, streets, streetcars, and subways. The Great Depression initiated a series of reforms that in time laid the groundwork for a postwar federally supported City. The process had begun with the collapse of several thousand banks and the private mortgage market during the thirties. The federal government rescued both sets of institutions by guaranteeing deposits placed in banks and offering mortgage insurance to homeowners, who were now to borrow according to the government's rules.

The federal emergency program grew out of President Hoover's 1931 National Conference on Home Building and Home Ownership. The Conference called for the diffusion of home ownership through American society as a panacea for slums and social unrest. To promote these goals it asked for the creation of long-term amortizing mortgages, low interest rates, direct aid to low-income families, and reduction of home construction costs. Beginning in 1933 the Home Owners' Loan Corporation (HOLC) introduced such mortgages. A year later the Federal Housing Administration (FHA) succeeded the HOLC and assumed the additional responsibilities of advocating for low interest rates and setting and enforcing construction standards designed to make housing less expensive.

The real estate, banking, and building industries pitted themselves against reformers seeking to launch further programs for housing low- and moderate-income families. These programs' supporters, "housers," as they were called, had emerged from campaigns for tenement house regulation and the experiments in worker housing undertaken for war workers in 1918. They hoped to adopt postwar European strategies for meeting the needs of the 60 percent of Americans who could not afford to purchase or rent new housing. Never in the history of the City had a majority been able to afford new construction, and to the housers this was an injustice.

The real estate, banking, and building interests, however, wielded significant political power because their industries were composed of thousands of local businesses and brokers spread across every Congressional district. The goal of this group was twofold. First, they wished to prevent any possible federal competition in the supply of low- to moderate-income housing, even though the private market had no ability to build new units for 60 percent of Americans. They did, however, wish to make permanent the role of the federal government as a supplier of inexpensive insured mortgages. Thus the Federal Housing Authority became the ally of private industry, and in time its practices came to reflect the biases of the private sector since its field agents regularly dealt with banks, land subdividers, and builders. In its leading and supporting roles the FHA codified the private practices of the day in its guidelines. In the interest of safety for its mortgage loans, its social rules favored class-graded neighborhoods and covenants to exclude Jews and African Americans, thus repeating the real estate industry's preferences.[5]

In 1937 the real estate lobby forced the "housers" into a corner: either accept a very narrowly restricted role for public housing or there would be no federal public housing program at all. The resulting Wagner-Steagall Act required that all public housing be subject to a tear-down rule; namely, every new unit built must be matched by the tearing down of a slum unit. In addition, all public housing should be built so economically that its structures would not compete with those of the private market. Public housing consequently became minimal housing for the poor. In the City it consisted of both high- and low-rise minimalist buildings set in superblocks arranged around communal green spaces and pathways and a few automobile-accessible streets.

Out of the 1937 compromise the United Sates' two-tiered housing programs emerged. There would be financial aid for private construction and an emphasis on single-family home ownership as opposed to rental units. In striking contrast, public housing managed by municipal departments would be strictly rationed by Congressional authorizations. The intention of the New Deal legislation was not antiurban, but the sum of its programs proved in time to be so.

Figure 7.4 Public housing, 1950. Since 1937 the federal government has made funding available for public housing; in dense urban areas entire neighborhoods were removed for the construction of large towers and low-rise blocks separated by parking areas and open space, after the models of Swiss modernist Le Corbusier. At the end of World War II, most of the projects' occupants were white veterans.

The federal government also stimulated suburban growth through utility improvements. As part of its public works stimulus program the federal government offered cost sharing for water and sewer improvements. In 1935 state commissioners identified a site for a major reservoir in a valley occupied by several small farming towns some eighty miles northwest of the City. A national grant funded the extension of the City's aqueduct to the new site. The rural lands around the valley were acquired for flooding and the protection of the watershed, the towns dissolved and their cemeteries moved to higher ground, and a dam was built. The completion of the reservoir and aqueduct in 1936 doubled the supply of water to the City and its surrounding suburbs. This program and the parallel federal aid for sewer improvement cost sharing in time fostered the speedy development of suburban land.

The most generous subsidy for decentralization, however, proved to be the income tax deductions for mortgages, local taxes, and depreciation. During and after World War II, when federal income taxes reached down to almost every citizen, these deductions rose in importance until they became the largest of all the federal subsidies for private building. Renters, of course, had no share in these benefits.[6]

These federal programs were coupled with a special set of measures designed to benefit the City's downtown real estate. Vacancies had inevitably followed the overbuilding of the 1920s real estate boom, and as the Depression came on rents sagged and the values of commercial properties declined. In response real estate firms and city planners began to envision a rebuilding of the inherited fabric of the central city. Perhaps the automobile could be better accommodated, parking spaces added, and traffic jams eliminated; perhaps old industrial properties could be cleared to make way for new towers-in-the-park designs; and perhaps warehouses, gasworks, breweries, and tenements next to the little-used wharves could be cleared for luxury apartments with beautiful harbor views. In the thirties, the National Association of Real Estate Boards and its urban subsidiary, the Urban Land Institute, perfected this idea, worked out an administrative structure, and secured several state authorizations for municipal boards that would devote themselves to what was then called "district planning" for redevelopment.[7]

These efforts confronted a conundrum: old commercial and tenement properties, even though they suffered low rent rolls, still commanded high center city land values. Despite the Depression, the cost of acquiring them one by one to make a large parcel exceeded the capabilities of private investors or the municipal treasury. The Urban Land Institute proposed a solution that would take the form of a federal subsidy to municipal "planning and redevelopment" agencies. The federal government would pay one-half or two-thirds of the cost of acquisition, and the municipal agencies would then write down the land values to sell the parcels cheaply to private developers. The Housing Acts of 1949 and 1954, although ostensibly oriented to public housing construction, adopted this ULI proposal in initiating an urban renewal program. Unfortunately, these statutes did not require that residents displaced by this process be found housing elsewhere at comparable rents.

Under the 1949 Housing Act, the federal government matched local funds two to one for the acquiring and rebuilding of areas local officials deemed "blighted." The term "blight" was an ostensibly economic term, as opposed to the social term "slum." The "blight" designation alleged that the property in question had lost its value as a productive economic investment, though there was inevitably class bias evident in its application. The City created a renewal agency that absorbed the planning department's zoning responsibilities and took on the job of locating and redeveloping blighted areas. The task proved slow and complicated. It took years for projects to qualify for federal funding, so the first fruits of the City's urban renewal took the form of empty cleared sites. In the process the public housing goals of the 1949 and 1954 Housing Acts got delayed and even lost. Nationally, between 1949 and 1968 a total of 425,000 units of housing had been cleared away and only 10,760 low-rent units constructed to replace them.[8]

In the suburbs of the City a number of housing experiments had been undertaken. During the war the government offered special incentives for residential development near the region's suburban defense plants and air strips, furthering the decentralizing pattern of population and industry. FHA Title VI regulations allowed developers to borrow 90 percent of their costs in advance in exchange for restricting sales to defense industry workers. This brought forth some of the largest residential developments in the region's history, and elements of their development and marketing set the trend for the next decades. The subdivisions contained four or five floor plans based on government suggestions for cost-efficient construction of healthy family environments.[9] Model homes, fully furnished, were publicized extensively in local newspapers. One newspaper called one of the larger wartime suburban developments of 15,000 homes "Residential development so extensive that it forms a remarkable chapter of its own in the history of our nation."[10]

The federal government attempted to ease the shortage of small apartments in the suburbs with its 608 Program. It offered 100 percent financing for developers who would erect "garden apartments," a low-rise, high-density form that had proved successful in England and in the United States during World War I. A number of builders, however, falsified their costs, and the program was shut down amid scandals four years later.

Despite these precedents, in the early postwar years the suburbs grew most commonly from the efforts of small builders who ran up modest Cape- and ranch-style single-family detached homes in groups of five and ten units. Near existing town centers they often also included some small apartment houses and

Figure 7.5 Suburbia, 1950. Over eight miles distant from downtown, developers laid out subdivisions of several thousand detached units. Their designs were based on FHA guidelines which called for grids modified by some curving streets and cul-de-sacs. On main arterials developers set aside land for commercial development, while schools were tucked into the interior of neighborhoods.

added a strip or two of stores. All of this early expansion depended on existing commuter rail lines, established arterial streets, and the occasional U.S. highways and retail clusters already in place.

A few builders experimented with new methods of construction, seeking to realize the possibilities of mass production by using a great deal of plywood, building on slabs of concrete, and prefabricating elements of houses. While the widespread use of the balloon frame had long allowed relatively quick development of freestanding wood-framed structures, now roof frames, fixtures, and even architectural details were built to industry standards promoted by the FHA. Private builders set up huge prefabrication operations for standardized units. One developer in 1947 bought a plot of 1,200 acres with a goal of 17,000 homes. He attempted to mass-produce homes of 800 square feet in the form of a one-story detached single-family house with an unfinished attic.[11] The heavy capital costs of such assembly-line methods for housing production, however, limited the success of the experiment. The real revolution in manufactured housing would come in the mid-1950s with the reinvention of the sports trailer as the ten-foot-wide mobile home, which could be delivered to a home site by truck and typically remain in that location. By the 1960s, single-wides and double-wides, almost entirely assembled in a factory, would prove the most efficient way to provide inexpensive homes.

THE PROSPERITY AND INEQUALITY OF THE PEOPLE

World War II also marked the beginning of an extended process of radical change in the long-standing residential arrangements of the City, thanks to an influx of new residents. Now the source of immigrants to the city shifted from Europe to Puerto Rico and the Caribbean. At the same time wartime employment drew African Americans from the south. In the 1950s, when the mechanical cotton picker became a practical machine and drove thousands off southern farms, this domestic migration attained the size of the late nineteenth century migrations. Already during the1940s, 483,000 African Americans had moved to the northeastern United States.[12]

The newcomers to the City, by necessity, settled into old low-rent areas of town, but when urban reconstruction got under way in the late 1950s many of these properties stood in the path of destruction for highways, urban renewal, and hospital and university projects. The sum of these clearances amounted to a loss of a large share of the City's cheap housing.

Well before the arrival of the bulldozers, the legal climate surrounding African American urban dwellers began to change. In 1941, at the outset of the world war, A. Philip Randolph of the Pullman Porters Union threatened a march on Washington to oppose segregation. In response, President Roosevelt issued an executive order banning racial discrimination in the hiring of workers on defense contracts. Despite this ruling, racial conflict broke out across the nation throughout the war, with major riots in Detroit over the hiring of African Americans. The armed forces of the nation remained segregated by race. Then in 1948 President Truman, following Roosevelt's earlier efforts, desegregated the armed forces.

The Supreme Court took an active role in hearing race cases. Following a series of decisions in 1948 the Supreme Court ruled in *Shelley v. Kramer* that racial covenants on land were unenforceable. Unfortunately the Federal Housing Administration and its associated agencies did not follow the thrust of this decision or its successor, *Brown v. Board of Education, Topeka, Kansas* (1954), that sought school desegregation. The FHA continued to approve mortgage insurance for developers who established whites-only communities. During the Eisenhower years, while much of the City's black middle class was on the move, their movement was mostly into "trickled down" housing on the fringes of traditionally black neighborhoods, with only a very small number of nonwhites gaining access to new housing.[13] President Kennedy brought the FHA's sponsorship of segregation to a close in 1962 when he issued his Executive Order 11063 to all federal departments, but even then discrimination in lending continued.[14]

For most non-minorities, the federal government's increased role from the 1930s to the early 1950s brought a prosperous, consumer-driven Cold War economy. In 1944 the Servicemen's Readjustment Act, commonly known as the GI Bill, offered veterans the possibility of purchasing a home with no money down and attaining college or vocational education. Banks could supply consumers with ample credit. Loans and mortgages were now accompanied by a new way for consumers to build debt: the credit card. In 1950 Diners Club came into being, which allowed customers to guarantee payment to multiple merchants with one card, and in 1958 both American Express and Visa were formed. Corporations offered fringe benefits for pensions and medical insurance. The middle class widely subscribed to "the Blues," as they were known: Blue Cross and Blue Shield.

Throughout the mid-twentieth century the area's middle class ballooned, investing in a lifestyle of amenities that most of their parents had never known. The City, now truly a metropolis of an aging urban core with its radiating and circumferential suburban attenuations, entered a new era of prosperity and change, albeit strained by tense postwar global conflicts and stubborn problems of class, race, and gender at home.

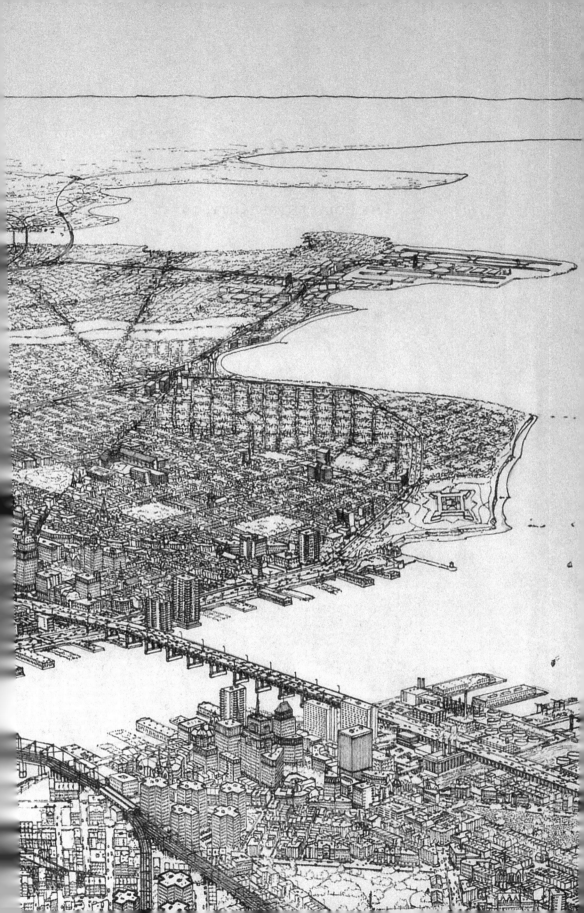

8

The Polycentric City, 1975

Figure 8.1   The City as it appeared in 1975.

By 1975 federal policy had transformed the geography of the City and its region. Private builders throughout the 1950s and 1960s, aided by risk-abating federal financial policies, responded to demand for home ownership. These policies allowed more and more people to purchase homes, transforming the City from a society of renters into one of owners. The building of freeways by federal planners after 1956 eliminated the centrality of the downtown, opening vast new areas to suburban residential and commercial development. While the population of the City shrank by 400,000 people to 1.6 million by 1975, the suburbs became home to 2.4 million people. Suburbanites now dominated the metropolis. Here and elsewhere suburbanites became the chief producers of American wealth and culture; products were tailored to their tastes and distributed, in image and actuality, around the entire world.

The widespread dispersal of homes and businesses realized a dream of housing reformers and planners who had for decades sought a green city to remedy tenements and urban crowding. Only thirty years before, such a metropolitan pattern as the one now in place had been the fantastic stuff of international exhibitions. Some academics and policymakers even saw in the now obsolete industrial areas interesting opportunities for urban rebuilding. The achievement of the new urban form came after years of prosperity.

These years also brought new difficulties. The civil rights movement began in the South and spread across the nation as southern African Americans migrated to northern cities seeking opportunities there. The federal government responded with far-reaching civil rights legislation in 1964. For the City, however, the demands of its African American citizens for full equality challenged deep racial divisions and called forth harsh political conflict and rioting. Encouraged by the civil rights movement, a dormant feminist movement revived during the 1960s and '70s to demand equal pay for women and to challenge the traditional gender patterns of white suburban society.

Postwar prosperity allowed the federal government to pursue a worldwide foreign policy that masked a growing dependence of the United States upon an ever more inclusive international economy. The Vietnam War (1957–1975) brought on inflation and rising costs of commodities and supplies. These costs in turn caused a painful rise in unemployment and some years of difficulty dubbed stagflation (a paradoxical combination of economic stagnation and inflation).

In 1973 the Organization of Petroleum Exporting Counties (OPEC) dramatically curtailed the supply of oil to the United States. The shock revealed the underlying weakness of the new polycentric metropolis: it depended on abundant inexpensive gasoline to make it function. Altogether, with the conflicts of Vietnam, civil rights, and the feminist movement, the seventies were a time of turmoil and unease, while the stagnation of the economy raised barriers to the hopes of progress that had captured the hearts of African Americans, women, and those seeking peace.

THE SHAPE OF THE POLYCENTRIC CITY

The landscape brought by postwar prosperity was highly uneven, reflecting the persistent inequalities of the day. The downtown declined as the suburban fringe developed; downtown's retail and commercial property, much of it now decades old, lost its appeal. The City's response to commercial disinvestment was an open-arms policy toward federal highway building and federal funds for development of housing, new office space, and civic buildings. Politicians in City Hall had the highest hopes for the federal highway program, initiated in 1956 under the National Interstate and Defense Highways Act.

Of all the forces at work, the new Interstate Highway program was the most powerful agent of change. The new highways of the 1960s were not like those built during the parkway years. The Interstates were six- to ten-lane toll-free roadways laid out for high-speed traffic, entirely free of at-grade intersections and served instead by massive interchanges. They were federally planned roads intended for interurban travel, and they did much more harm to the City than help.[1] Interstate routes were constructed to repeat the spiderweb pattern of the railroad lines that fanned outward from the center. Upon the completion of these inbound-outbound lines a few circumferential Interstates were added to the network, leading to a vast amount of regional intrasuburban traffic.

Highway construction resulted in displacement of long-time residents. A single highway project required the seizure of thousands of properties through eminent domain and the removal of five, ten, or, in the case of the massive central interchange and expressway on the north side of downtown, as many as twenty thousand people. These actions galvanized community opposition, and in the late 1960s two cross-town highways were canceled as a result of the local "freeway revolt." Most of the network, however, was completed as planned.

Though local officials hoped highway access and abundant parking structures would draw business to downtown, these just as easily ensured a way to leave the City as a way to get there. Urban expressways hastened the decentralization of the metropolis and the loss of the office-store-theater downtown's dominance. The peripheral beltways that were built as part of the Interstate system allowed drivers to circumnavigate the City, and new freeway arterials allowed land speculation distant from the City. Where these arterials met the beltways, developers planned massive subdivisions, shopping centers, and office parks distant from traditional centers, enhancing the region's polycentric form.

With the shift in transit to the private automobile, the state consolidated the ownership of the regional rail, streetcar, and subway networks from the near-bankrupt private companies that operated them. The great train stations of earlier decades entered into decay as intercity travel became dominated by the automobile and airplane. The new state transportation authority did, however, take several measures to end decreases in ridership. It replaced streetcars with buses that could more easily navigate automobile-dominated streets. In the 1970s, with the arrival of federal funding, some subway stations were improved and modernized, and a few subway lines were extended to the City's fringe where large park-and-ride garages were built, promoting use of the network by suburbanites.

The city government took extreme measures to maintain what was left of the downtown's regional weight in the now metropolitan commercial real estate market. Encouraged by the funding for renewal of the Housing Acts of 1949 and 1954, the City reorganized its planning office to undertake urban renewal clearance and reconstruction. The City took aim at working-class residential districts on the fringes of downtown, labeling them "blighted." Many of the residences condemned were fully occupied, maintained, and appreciated by their residents. In the most unfortunate cases, blocks of residences were seized, razed, and the land redeveloped for consumers wealthier than the former occupants. Charles Abrams, long a champion of low-income housing, estimated the clearance in Baltimore to be the equivalent of the wartime bombing of a European city.[2] Because of the choice of targets, this tearing down came to be criticized as "Negro Removal" by civil rights activists. Many of the boardinghouses on the immediate north and west sides of downtown were razed. Transients and the underemployed became underhoused; the City dealt with this problem by rigidly sequestering services for the homeless adjacent to

Chinatown on the City's near north side. Here a postwar skid row of homeless shelters, gambling parlors, brothels, and drug pushers was shielded from downtown by the City's new ten-lane east-west expressway.

Planners aimed to fill razed areas with a mix of private corporate towers, high-rise apartments, and public buildings. Unfortunately, some areas simply became parking lots because it took years to solicit private companies interested in building new developments that could transform the City's skyline and guarantee growing tax revenues.

The progressive ideals of past decades' public housing advocates had unforeseen outcomes in the 1970s. Since the 1930s the City had accepted federal money for public housing that it imagined would provide an attractive, modern alternative to the City's aging housing stock. At first, most occupants were gainfully employed persons, often World War II veterans, who used the housing as a temporary stepping-stone as they saved money for home purchases elsewhere. By the 1970s, however, this mix of utilitarian-looking tower block and low-rise housing, sprinkled throughout the City's old residential neighborhoods, sheltered the underemployed and low-wage workers, many of whom were recent arrivals from the South, or families removed by renewal schemes. With a shrinking local job market in manufacturing and few or no services for adult job training, a culture of dependency settled upon these vertical ghettos. In 1975 the largest of these "projects," as they were commonly known, had a population of nearly 10,000, over 50 percent of whom were unemployed and 80 percent dependent on public assistance.[3]

This era of heavy-handed city building did have some beneficial impacts. Along the waterfront abandoned warehouses were condemned, parks and apartments were built, and the public was given access to a now quieter and well-maintained harbor. Downtown civic projects and public-private partnership projects did in time work to stem the outward tide of commercial investment. During the sixties and seventies the finance, health care, and education sectors of the economy expanded and took their places in a downtown now refurbished for corporate comfort.

The design of many of the renewal projects was, however, questionable. It often produced stark modernist landscapes of broad, treeless, windswept plazas framed by concrete civic structures or glass corporate towers. By the 1970s the construction of several unpopular downtown renewal projects had brought growing opposition to eminent domain and the associated disruption of

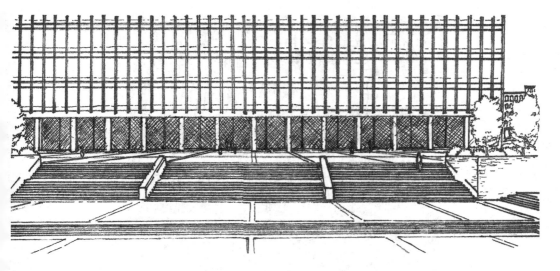

Figure 8.2 Downtown Federal Building and Plaza, 1975. Postwar urban renewal schemes led to the rescue of downtown commercial values, but through unpopular legal means and design that failed to live up to expectations. Busy multimodal streets and neighborhoods were replaced by government and commercial buildings with limited ground-floor activity and mostly barren pedestrian plazas.

neighborhoods. At the same time the slowing of funds from a cash-strapped Washington led the City's renewal agency and other authorities to cut back. More serious for the City, many of the federal programs for subsidized construction of low- and moderate-rent housing were so tainted with fraud that in 1973 President Nixon closed all subsidized housing activities and the next year replaced them with direct grants of rent to low-income tenants, the so-called Section 8 grants.

Beyond the borders of the City, the suburbs continued to grow. The largest suburban subdivisions, built by well-financed development corporations, became new self-governing municipalities with their own neighborhood shopping centers and schools. Other suburbs burgeoned as centers for employment and also became regional shopping and entertainment destinations.

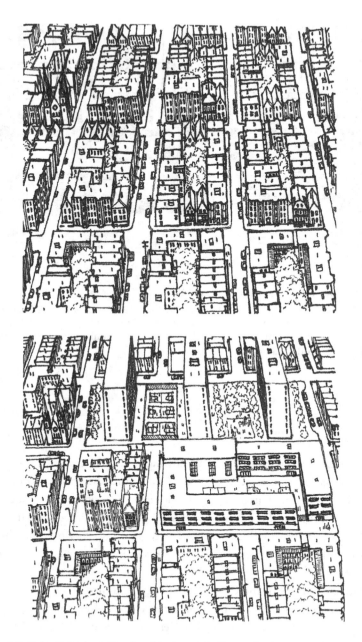

Figures 8.3, 8.4 Urban neighborhood before and after renewal, 1950 and 1975. Renewal frequently involved the destruction of the intimate scale of the city's streetcar buildouts, and the superimposing of so-called superblocks onto the street pattern. Here several streets have been removed to make way for plazas and playgrounds between high-rises and a new school.

Older suburbs filled out their last remaining undeveloped areas with large spacious ranch and colonial style homes. Often these suburbs used exclusionary zoning regulations to fend off a feared influx of modestly priced houses that would offer low tax returns. In this politically fragmented, sprawling, and polycentric urban region, suburbanites preferred to think of themselves as living detached, socially and spatially, from what many of them understood to be a crime-ridden, semivacant relic of a bygone era just a few exits down the Interstate.

Independence from the core City increased each year with new suburban employment, shopping, and entertainment options. Beginning in the 1960s, the City's universities opened suburban medical and research complexes ten to fifteen miles from the City's center to serve suburban workers. A significant federal investment in defense- and public-health-related research helped the City's fringe to garner new high-tech industries in health and engineering. One freeway became commonly known as "Tech Alley" in the 1970s and has kept that moniker ever since. Veterans of university or federal laboratories founded new companies in electronics, aerospace, medical device manufacturing, chemical research, and material sciences. These new industries replaced the region's heavy industry, and many workers followed manufacturing jobs out of the region. In their stead, middle-class, college-educated employees migrated into the region for high-paying jobs in the new industries. As a whole the region became wealthier and costlier. The new industries, however, could never fully take the place of the old manufacturing base; even combined with the region's growing service sector, they failed to attract anything like the urban in-migration of previous decades. At a time when metropolises in California and the South were doubling in size over twenty years, the City and its metropolitan region grew at a modest pace of 10 percent a decade; its population reached 4 million by 1980. Its economic output grew only slightly faster.

Suburban municipalities competed among themselves for retail tax revenue from businesses migrating from the City. Hoping for a tax revenue bonanza, suburban areas zoned graciously for commercial uses. Auto dealerships, roadside motels, drive-through restaurants, and gas stations multiplied along suburban strips to take advantage of the infinite frontage of the highway.[4] The shopping malls and the strips together revolutionized suburban form, changing it from a more traditional pattern of concentrated nodes of activity to one of linear strips and far-flung centers.

Though one-story commercial strips had been common since the early twentieth century, they were now almost always set back from the street by parking areas. The first such plaza was built in the region in 1951, and a hundred more followed by the end of the decade. Department stores added branches in suburban locations convenient to automobile-dependent shoppers, and closed downtown flagship stores. In suburbs the department stores now acted as anchors for new indoor shopping centers. The first such indoor mall was built in the region in 1959. It featured one large anchor department store and twenty smaller stores. To accommodate this tax-lucrative development, towns passed parking requirements for new commercial establishments that required enough parking area so that even during the Christmas rush every shopper could find an empty spot. Multiacre parking lots became common sights around the largest shopping plazas. Shoppers became so accustomed to free parking that traditional town centers declined. The small-scale credit-granting grocery of old suburban town centers made way for large cash-only chain groceries surrounded by parking lots. These new grocery stores sold store and brand name goods at low prices. Many handsome commercial structures in older suburban centers fell vacant; owners of aging commercial properties across the region often found they could make money off their commercial properties only by demolishing them and using the land for surface parking. The City and suburbs alike invested in countless municipal parking structures to compete for shoppers and workers.

The construction of the federal highway system also led to the suburbanization of the region's distribution industry. Trucking had been on the rise and was a major reason for federal investment in road building since the First World War, but it was now a highly competitive mode of shipping in the region and nationally.[5] Nondescript warehouses sprouted on the suburban fringes. Railroad freight companies opened suburban facilities to ease intermodal movement of goods between train and truck. Many warehouses downtown were shuttered, and those associated with the movement of goods inland by water also closed as the amount of waterway traffic in the region stagnated.

Five major malls opened in the region in the 1960s and 1970s, four at interchanges on the beltway surrounding the City. The largest featured 150 tenants, three of which were department stores. The fifth and smallest was built downtown in 1972 by a public-private partnership, where it struggled beneath losses for nearly twenty years. All of the new malls featured air-conditioning. In the suburbs five movie multiplexes had opened by the mid-1970s. The first opened in 1960 with three screens. In 1970 two of the five regional multiplexes had ten screens. Downtown theaters shut or turned to pornographic uses.

While life inside the average household may have been one of increased convenience, it was more difficult to argue that the public realm had similarly benefited. The daily frustrations of previous generations of rail and streetcar commuters gave way to new ones. Massive two- or three-story structures of concrete, known from their shape as cloverleaf or stacked-diamond interchanges, became the source of modern commuters' headaches. While the smoke that belched from nineteenth-century smokestacks was largely gone by the late 1960s, automobiles, refrigerators, and air conditioners produced a new array of air pollutants with their own unique health and ecological consequences. Increased consumption also fostered landscapes far less attractive than the local indoor mall: the waste landfill. Some of the City's wharves found new life as sites for shipping waste to underwater landfills. One wharf company simply tore down its obsolete facilities and built a landfill right on the harbor.

So much consumption demanded electricity. Power companies built three major facilities in suburban areas in the decades after World War II. One of these was a nuclear power plant, at a distance of forty miles from the City's center. While location of hazardous uses in urban areas met with minimal public resistance due to the residents' lack of political clout, in the suburbs the plants hastened the nation's nascent environmental movement. Though often out of self-interest, wealthy suburbanites lobbied their town halls to resist placement of waste dumps or power-generating facilities in their territory. Airport expansion was also a contentious issue. The result was usually the placement of unwanted land uses in rural locations or poor urban areas, where local governments welcomed the tax revenue they generated and ordinary citizens were left to deal with the negative environmental consequences. In time the necessity for such facilities was brought into question, and debate surrounding renewable energy sources slowly began. Under the Nixon Administration the environmental movement gained national traction with the Clean Water Act, the Clean Air Act, and the establishment of the Environmental Protection Agency. Locally this meant the mitigation of many public health and ecological hazards as industries were forced to reduce the release of pollutants. Still, however, various public health risks remained highest among the minorities and poor who could not afford to move away from major polluters, or force polluters to stay away from them.

Beyond the downtown commercial area, in the old inner working-class neighborhoods, the midcentury period of war and ensuing prosperity erased the loyalties of the younger generation of whites to their ethnic enclaves and many former traditions. Leaving familial and religious differences behind in the social mixing of wartime, many Polish, Italian, Greek, and Irish Americans intermarried and established new lives in the suburbs. No longer divided by competition for wage labor and parochial loyalties, many in the region's Catholic majority entered into the area's middle and upper classes. With new homes and new ways, the old political rivalries between wealthy, suburban, Republican Anglo-Protestants in and working-class, urban, Democratic Catholics softened. In racial terms, the City's postwar order consisted of an ethnically mixed, prosperous white majority, a shrinking urban white working class, and a mostly urban, isolated, growing African American minority. What remained of the white working class in the City was also marginalized in the new suburban American culture, and continued to look down on their African American urban counterparts whom they considered to be their competition for low-wage manufacturing jobs and political power.

The City's African American population grew rapidly as mechanization of farm labor spurred a fresh wave of African American immigration. Urban whites blamed African Americans for the decay of urban neighborhoods, which in reality stemmed from a nest of causes: "white flight," the limited economic opportunities facing the many newcomers in a deindustrializing City, discriminatory hiring and discriminatory public and private lending practices, the disruption caused by urban renewal, and neglect by absentee landlords. The City's politicians also remained unwilling and unable to accommodate the newcomers and to deal with the problems of minority neighborhoods. Instead they continued to contract out public services to friends and allies, often neglecting minority neighborhoods and shutting out minority-owned firms.

The examples of the integration of the armed forces during the Korean and Vietnam wars and the general prosperity of the white metropolis encouraged northern urban African Americans to join the civil rights movement. The gains of the movement in the arena of political equality, however, did not easily translate into economic and social equality. The Fair Housing Act of 1968 made discriminatory lending and renting practices illegal, but the discriminatory practices of small banks and landlords remained difficult to detect because they were often simply disguised under other criteria. White urban boss-politicians, loyal to their white constituents, continued to tolerate or promote discriminatory practices by local banks, and African American civil organizations lacked the finances to pursue even a small minority of cases.

Banks thus continued to pursue policies of redlining, refusing to grant mortgages to African American homebuyers outside of certain areas the FHA had specified. The areas where African Americans did attain home ownership were ones with the oldest housing stock, far from the suburbs with their new construction and independent school districts. As a result, African Americans remained an overwhelmingly urban population in the industrial north.[6] A disproportionately high number of them were renters, and many of the remainder owned houses of declining value. Whereas in previous decades the term "ghetto" had been applied to a few ethnic neighborhoods, by the 1960s it became synonymous with urban black America in the minds of African Americans and whites alike.

The Fair Housing Act also sped up the pace of white flight from the City. In a practice called "blockbusting," white real estate agents convinced white property owners that loans to African American buyers in their neighborhood would lead to boarded-up houses, arson, and violent crime. Whites sold at low prices and moved. In one local case, a minority advocacy group filed suit to stop white homeowners from placing outdoor "for sale" signs on their properties, stating that this accelerated the pace of blockbusting, but here and across the country courts found such arguments to be without merit.[7] The predatory brokers then convinced corrupt FHA officials to assess homes at many times the market value, selling them to African American families with a very low down payment, only to foreclose on them shortly thereafter when they became saddled with debts they could not pay. Many homes were left abandoned in this way. Both frustrated buyers struggling with mortgage debt and owners of run-down properties turned to arson to collect insurance. In 1975 an average of five acts of arson were committed in the City each night, mostly on residential properties, by a mix of vandals, persons in arson-for-profit insurance schemes, and landlords.[8]

The assassination of Martin Luther King Jr. in 1968 and the ensuing riots, followed by the militarization of elements of the civil rights movement, led to further misunderstanding and fears among whites. In 1971 the Supreme Court in *Swann v. Charlotte-Mecklenburg Board of Education* upheld the strategy of

Figure 8.5 Neighborhood abandonment, 1975. The acts of redlining and blockbusting led to the abandonment of older areas and their abuse by arson schemes and gangs. As much of the middle class suburbanized and businesses left, remaining residents were left with a derelict, trash-ridden, discouraging landscape in which to live.

promoting racial integration by forming integrated schools. In 1972 an African American organization won a legal battle by proving the City's school system to be intentionally segregated. The group presented the case of an African American boy living in a majority white school district who had been assigned to a majority African American school three miles away. The City responded with a policy of busing for all students. Riots broke out. Buses of African American schoolchildren were stoned as they entered white neighborhoods. When police escorts ensured the safety of African American students, white schoolchildren stopped attending. In the following years many white families moved to suburban areas rather than have their children attend integrated schools, or they placed their children in religious schools. By 1980 the City's school system had an African American majority even though whites still comprised a majority of the City's population.

The result of white flight was immediately apparent to the City's African Americans. Many now lived in neighborhoods where property ownership was in fact a poor investment; absentee white owners shuttered businesses and streets were depopulated. For the first time in the City's history, houses stood abandoned and dilapidated in many neighborhoods. Weeds and garbage filled vacant lots. With the eyes of residents off the street, urban neighborhoods became increasingly dangerous places for all. For City Hall population decline and disinvestment in property meant a declining tax base. Schools were closed and the remaining ones became overcrowded. Burned-out homes and vacant lots attracted squatters and crime. The polycentric metropolis, it became clear, meant a dispersed regional settlement pattern with areas of deep economic disadvantage.

Only a few miles from the ghetto, the lifestyles of the new suburbanites were a world apart from those in the older City center in terms of consumption, daily habits, and opportunities. The City engaged a smaller and smaller proportion of suburbanites' attention: many visited only for work purposes, if that. The City's suburbanites were among the wealthiest people in the nation. Things considered luxuries one year could in five years become mass-produced items within the reach of the general public. Such was the case for televisions in the 1950s, dishwashers, driers, and washing machines in the 1960s, and microwaves in the 1970s. Residents also consumed more space and traveled more miles per day than they ever had. By the mid-1970s there was one car for every two persons in the region; one television and one telephone for every 2.5 persons; and the average person purchased twice what their parents had every year in terms of clothing and household items such as kitchenware, decor, and linens. In 1975 nearly all households in the region had a refrigerator, while half of them owned a refrigerator with a built-in freezer, 40 percent owned a dishwasher, and three-quarters owned a washing machine.[9] Such figures were matched by only a few other regions in the United States, and none outside it.

In 1973 an oil embargo brought great stress to this sprawling metropolitan region. Unfortunately, during and since that crisis, politics focused on restoring the means to continue established habits, rather than encouraging the adoption of new ones. Bargains were made and the cheap gasoline returned for a while. The combined effects of the embargo, the Vietnam War, and the increased globalization of industrial production, however, were enough to drive the country into recession. The failure of the peace and free speech movements to

Figure 8.6   Raised ranch, 1975. In the 1960s and 1970s this style of split-level became prevalent in the suburbs of the City. An exterior set of stairs led up to the front door, which opened onto a small foyer halfway between the two main floors of the house.

bring about a timely end to an unpopular war led many to turn inward. The young increasingly shunned political action or their parents' ideals of personal responsibility and turned their attention to media culture. For a time in the 1970s and the years of recession a college education seemed to be of minimal economic benefit.[10]

The wealth of many of the region's households during the seventies was only maintained by waves of wives and mothers entering the workforce. For most working-class and middle-class families during the sixties the earnings of one worker had sufficed. Now, with the stagnating economy and the decline in union-protected jobs, only a two-earner family generally had any hope of achieving a high standard of living.

Drug use expanded among all classes but most markedly among the poor. Perhaps out of unrealizable expectations of economic growth and social and cultural development, a new culture of individualism and distrust arose, represented by a barrage of cliché labels: tree-huggers, hippies, punks, squares, and Jesus freaks. Liberal and conservative became loaded terms on radio talk shows and around dinner tables. Spatially, culturally, and economically divided, the region moved on with low self-esteem and limited appreciation for the relative stability of its institutions, in a world ridden with poverty, violence, and civil strife the likes of which most in this City would never know.

9

THE GLOBAL CITY, 2000

Figure 9.1   The City as it appeared in 2000.

A City of the World

By the first decade of the new millennium the City had reinvented itself with a new economy, a new culture, and most obviously new forms. The City's center became a media subject. Local newspapers and magazines featured articles titled "City Life Is Back" and "The Urban Renaissance." Four television sitcoms of the 1990s based on the lifestyles of young, single, usually white urban professionals were set in fictional loft condominiums, restored Victorian row houses, and downtown office towers of the City. Hollywood released several films in that decade featuring romances and adult comedy set in the City—a far departure from the industry's exploitation of the City's mafia dramas and ghettos in the 1970s and 1980s.

Powerful public and private marketers promoted the City as a hot spot for world-dominating economic and artistic creativity. They pointed to this global culture's emblems of success, stamped on the world from Toronto to Singapore: an international population, luxury hotels catering to world travelers, global influence in finance and the arts, sleek new monuments to international corporations, and downtown and suburban shopping and gallery areas packed with the output of world-renowned artists and designers.

While this image prevailed in the minds of local boosters, business travelers, tourists, and many of the region's youth, the selectivity of their views belied a complex reality. The city proper had gained 100,000 residents in the last two decades of the twentieth century, but the vast majority of population and employment growth continued to locate in the City's suburban areas. The central parts of the City revived as homes for professionals, artists, young transients, and new immigrants. The rebirth in these districts, however, often came at a social and economic cost to long-time residents. In the 2000s the City and its suburbs suffered a level of economic inequality not seen since the 1920s.[1]

The departure of manufacturing jobs for other regions, the disintegration of unions, and the thrust of the new economy widened the gap between those with and without college educations and weakened the position of the working and middle classes. Also, many routine back office jobs in accounting, finance, insurance, and computer servicing shifted to low-wage English-speaking countries in the Third World. The new global culture of the City and its suburbs revealed itself to be the culture of the prosperous educated class.

Electronic innovation aided the region in replacing some number of stable blue- and white-collar jobs. In the 1970s and 1980s the City became a center for the manufacture of computer hardware, and in time this line of products gave way to software innovations. As a research center, the City also specialized in the manufacture of health care machinery and devices. Hospitals and clinics multiplied by offering previously unknown interventions, and drug manufacture grew to new proportions. Mutual fund and pension fund management grew to be a trillion dollar local specialty.

Likewise new inventions in financial marketing, including derivative trading, enabled investment houses and banks to expand rapidly. By 2000 the successful and expanding industries of the City also depended on an equally new and growing workforce of service workers—medical and computer repair, hotel and hospital staffing, food service, services to homes such as school teaching, day care, landscaping, and local government—all the myriad tasks that the newly prosperous demanded.

Although many of these activities required a highly educated workforce, state government responded perversely to the recessions of the 1970s and 1980s by cutting back funding for community colleges and the state university. These institutions then raised their tuition charges, heightening the barriers to higher education for working-class and middle-class children.

The Form of the Global City

The transformations in the City's economy manifested themselves in a scattered geography of new architectural forms. The modest diner and hamburger stand were followed by a regional scattering of fast-food franchises; the former apartments placed over the Main Street stores in streetcar and railroad suburbs were followed by considerable clusters of three- and four-story apartments along suburban arterial roads; a floor or two no longer sufficed for the downtown corporation as it required much of a tower to itself; hospitals sprouted new wings, ancillary research buildings, and suburban satellites; colleges and universities seeking evening and weekend tuitions imitated the suburbanizing hospitals.

These physical elements in turn mirrored the new institutional patterns of a culture of corporations: business corporations, hospital corporations, universities, large regional school districts, nonprofit land conservation corporations, ever more and larger golf clubs and marinas, ever larger fund drives for the symphony and the art museum.

Land was not spared. Encouraged by local planning boards and generous mortgage financing, the typical subdivision grew from ten or fewer acres to a planned unit development of several hundred. In these large developments builders placed suburban apartments near the arterial roads and malls, set the single-family houses in the interior, and placed town houses strategically next to the reserved open spaces, golf clubs, and swimming pools. The regional mall of large and small stores sat at an interchange, surrounded by gigantic parking lots. Higher-end malls perhaps symbolized the global City best, with their displays of luxuries that had been harvested worldwide and now set out in retail islands located next to the region's highway nodes.

In keeping with the growth of consumer culture, the City once again became a major center for the distribution of cargo. The City's prominence in air shipping grew when a new Airport Authority improved airports to accommodate the movement of goods by air nationally and internationally. The proliferation of commercial jet travel in the 1970s and 1980s also led the Airport Authority to invest heavily in new airline terminals. The City's major airport became a hub for several domestic carriers, international flights to Europe in the 1980s, and by the late 1990s to Asia and Latin America as well.

To respond to the standardization of international shipping containers for transport by boat, truck, and rail, the state established a Port Authority to manage the modernization of the City's port. The port also grew with the expansion of oil and gas consumption. It daily received tankers from abroad, and the expansion of its south side refineries established the City as a minor center for the energy industry. The Port Authority extended many wharves and erected large cranes to accommodate purpose-built container ships. The state also built a new rail corridor exclusively for freight between the port and a suburban warehouse district. The resurgence of goods distribution in the City and the region provided a base for stable working-class jobs in trucking and warehousing at a time when most new jobs in the region were opening only for those with college educations and professional degrees.

The refurbishment of the downtown and some of its nearby districts symbolized a new era of wealth and global influence at the top: a revived downtown, but less as a true center for the metropolis than a playground for the rich, the corporate, and the hip. The renewal projects of the 1960s and 1970s, despite their controversial nature, paid off in improved real estate values. From the mid-1970s to the late 1990s the downtown enjoyed a series of commercial building booms. A growing presence of permanent downtown residents in a number of new high-rise condominium towers and converted loft spaces in obsolete commercial buildings added a welcome new element for the City's center.

In the 1990s the City engaged in a policy of recreating downtown as a 24-hour district, subsidizing restaurants and retail, rezoning for residential development, and relaxing building codes for adaptive reuse of old commercial and industrial properties. The waterfront also reemerged as a recreational destination. Resembling suburban gated communities, the new condominium towers of downtown and the waterfront were vertical controlled communities, offering residents the privacy and security of a suburban existence along with proximity to a very heavily marketed and polished conception of downtown living. The occupants varied: some were young, single professionals, others childless couples. Some wealthy families who educated their children at private schools joined them, as did well-to-do retirees from suburban areas looking to downsize to locations proximate to cultural activities. Because the number of residents and daytime workers grew once more, downtown retail began a recovery during the 1980s. New department stores, high-fashion boutiques, electronics stores, and restaurants opened in traditional shopping districts. A controversial downtown mall project of the early 1970s was refashioned to allow more direct access to the street.

In the old neighborhoods surrounding downtown, beginning in the late 1970s, young "urban pioneers," many of them white gay persons and artists, began moving into the nineteenth-century row houses, gradually displacing much of the working-class population that had lived there for many decades. These neighborhoods became known for their cultural variety and for their marketing as gritty, urban "cool" places. In time this first wave of gentrifiers was gradually replaced by yet another wealthier set of professionals.

The preservationist movement added an unlooked-for novelty after decades of modernization. In response to the destructive impacts of urban renewal and the dismissal of traditional neighborhoods by contemporary planners, various groups sought to enhance the City's vitality by preserving its historic built environment. The first victories involved the preservation of large public monuments, namely the City Hall, which by the 1970s was being described by some city officials as archaic. When the latter proposed a measure to replace the building, it was rebuffed by Council members sympathetic to the preservationist cause. In the 1980s City Council approved the creation of two historic

Figures 9.2, 9.3 Downtown scene, 1975 and 2000. Commercial values downtown plummeted in the immediate postwar years. Stores of all sizes closed and office space was abandoned. Many buildings were torn down to make way for parking lots, as this was often a more profitable use. The ghosts of lost structures remain visible on the sides of their former abutters, where indications of their masonry are visible. Twenty-five years later, the parking lot pictured in the 1975 view has been replaced by a boutique technology store, and adjacent commercial buildings converted to lofts or flexible office space. Sidewalks have been widened and planted with trees, bump-outs and curb cuts added, and bus shelters installed.

preservation districts in a pair of the City's old residential districts. Construction projects in these areas, if performed on existing structures, were required not to alter the exterior of the building; new structures had to be proportional to existing structures and use traditional materials.

Subsequent to this initial preservation effort, community groups successfully pressed City Hall for the creation of an African American historical district, a Waterfront Historic Walk, a Jewish Heritage Trail, and other culturally oriented preservation and educational efforts. A defunct mill was reopened as a museum of the nineteenth-century textile industry, and a World War II-era destroyer was opened as a naval museum. By the late 1990s funds for adaptive reuse of existing structures were available in many designated low-income areas of the City, but they also carried with them the impact of rising costs.

Spurred by European examples, the City also launched a campaign against the automobile, saying it detracted from the pedestrian experience of the City and created empty sidewalk spaces of too much noise and air pollution. The pedestrianization of some heavily themed downtown shopping districts ensued. A national movement in architecture and planning dubbed "new urbanism" led to the design of transit- and pedestrian-friendly developments in the City and its suburbs. These developments featured a mixing of uses and unit types and the use of traditional architecture; despite generally smaller lot and unit sizes, their offering of commercial and recreational amenities in proximity to residences allowed them to command a high price point. Thus, despite the new urbanists' emphasis on remaking the built environment for all, their projects were only accessible to the few.

By 2000 many City neighborhoods boasted improved sidewalks, sidewalk plantings, bump-outs, curb cuts, raised crossings, bicycle lanes, and other measures aimed to make the City friendlier to multiple modes of transportation. The City financed attractive glass shelters at bus stops by having advertisers maintain the shelters. Such measures also had a positive impact on the economy of the City's neighborhoods in promoting sidewalk sociability, safety, and commercial activity.

In conformity with the times, large institutions and corporations made their mark on the City in the late twentieth century. Consolidation in the health care industry in the 1980s and 1990s led many hospitals to expand their facilities and build new laboratories and clinics in the City and suburbs, creating large central medical clusters with regional satellites. In the 1990s two new civic buildings, a museum of contemporary art and a concert hall, opened on the waterfront on opposite sides of the river. Major corporations built two new office towers downtown that were more than 800 feet tall and one in excess of 1,000 feet, a new tallest that dramatically altered the skyline.

The City also succeeded with two large public-private revitalization projects on the edges of downtown. The first was the conversion of the old baseball stadium into a historic site and artistic venue, complemented by the construction of a convention and shopping center on the abutting parking areas. A new baseball stadium was built near Union Station.

These recreational, retail, office, and residential opportunities downtown boosted the area's image and led to significant growth in tourism and business conventions. Four- and five-star hotel chains opened several new locations downtown and in adjacent neighborhoods. The City financed new crosswalks, tree plantings, and sidewalk and lighting improvements throughout downtown. Business owners in the downtown and a few adjacent neighborhoods formed business improvement districts by levying an assessment on themselves to pay for further security and maintenance by private service providers. By 2000 the only vestiges of the City's industrial past visible downtown were in the cast-iron facades of warehouses that now masked lofts and refurbished office space.

What some saw as a welcome rebirth others criticized as a corporatizing of downtown. Some also resented downtown's growing exclusivity: both in its increased lack of affordability for many city residents and in the explicit corralling of the homeless and other undesirables into smaller pockets near shelters and other service facilities. The City's homeless population increased over the course of the 1970s, '80s, and '90s as veterans' benefits were trimmed, state mental facilities closed, and the City razed abandoned buildings to fight crime that it associated with squatters. One business improvement district did operate a shelter for the homeless of its area as part of a strategy that could benefit both the homeless and business owners, but this was an exceptional case.

Many traditional populations of inner-city neighborhoods also found themselves on the move. With the rapid influx of well-to-do newcomers who discouraged the addition of affordable housing options in their newfound communities, various less-advantaged groups defined by wealth, age, ethnicity, or sexual identity played hopscotch around the City's neighborhoods. The poor were especially disadvantaged in this succession. They had to crowd into rental units in inner-city areas ill served by public transit. In their newfound cleanliness, safety, and appeal to a mainstream set, some said that downtown and its near neighborhoods had attained the sterile character of suburbia. Many more people in the region, however, saw little to dislike in this change.

Meanwhile the suburbs themselves continued to change. Both in function and demographic makeup, the City's suburbs since the 1980s increasingly defied the popular image of the American bedroom community as the exclusive territory of the white middle and upper classes.

Some inner suburban areas absorbed much of the poverty being forced out of the City proper by rising land values there. Their municipal tax bases stagnant and their school systems unequipped to deal with so many rapid demographic changes, these municipalities had more in common with the City in its most stressful periods than with their suburban counterparts. Many successfully rescued themselves from financial ruin by converting former industrial property to commercial use. By 2000 the inner-ring suburbs were home to some of the region's largest big-box stores. The tax revenues raised allowed these communities to maintain an adequate level of services and civil peace.

The railroad commuter suburbs that had developed as middle- or upper-middle-class towns held on staunchly to their identity. Strict zoning codes severely limited new construction; property values remained high and the number of new families few. By popular agreement these suburbs were among the most attractive parts of the region in which to live because of their services and proximity to the City's employment centers. Ironically, by the end of the 1990s their exclusivity began to turn on them. Because few young families could afford houses here, the population aged and the communities lost their child-centered life. With little new construction the tax base stagnated, schools closed, trick-or-treaters became an endangered species, and residential property taxes climbed to support the level of public services residents had always demanded.

In response, some of these towns did open themselves up to revenue-generating commercial uses and some affordable housing. New commercial districts were added to town centers, and parts of the old turnpikes leading out of the City became automobile versions of the former streetcar commercial street. Other towns channeled development into areas near their commuter rail stations, revitalizing traditional town centers with residential and new commercial uses. Elsewhere citizen groups in some wealthy inner suburbs were able to resist even the smallest changes in their towns.

The accumulating list of regulations in many established communities heightened the desirability of building in distant fields and forests of the region where rural towns imposed few regulations. Lenders were happy to support such placements, even with questionable lending practices. Developers laid out spacious subdivisions with broad winding streets, cul-de-sacs, and large homes. Their design responded both to middle-class expectations and automobile-oriented subdivision codes that called for ever-wider streets and larger turn radiuses. The City's region sprawled, and now featured more land per person on average than at any time in its history.[2]

The newest suburbs overwhelmed the capacity of Interstate highways and state routes at rush hour. Former rural roads pressed into service as feeder lines seized up with the morning and evening commutes, but traffic lights and widening and new interchanges relieved the worst problems.

In this outer area at the interchanges of Interstates and once-rural roads, "edge cities" sprang up, presenting themselves as alternatives for businesses not willing to pay for a downtown address. Eventually, even some large corporations took advantage of the suburbs' low prices. By the opening of the new millennium at least half of the metropolitan region's employment, and a similar share of its population, lay at least fifteen miles from downtown. So much suburban growth meant that downtown, despite its revival, remained a small part of the regional economy. Only an eighth of all commuters in the region spent their daytime there in 2000, a figure that confounded regional public transportation planners.

The edge cities were not all big-box stores, traffic, outlet malls, and office parks. In these outer suburbs some developers sought out new ways to manufacture familiar settings. They built several new outdoor shopping centers, called "lifestyle centers," designed to imitate a suburban village and to call up associations of easy small-town sociability. These were open-air malls mimicking a pedestrian, antique streetscape. The surrounding large parking lots however, challenged the illusion; in fact, these developments were just as auto-dependent as their enclosed predecessors.

Gated communities added to this menu of idyllic suburbia. Furnished with gatehouses, loaded with restrictive covenants, their names evoking some bucolic paradise, they multiplied exponentially in the 1980s. Developers also cooked up other specialized packages for suburban settlers: 55-and-older settlements, subdivisions centered on boating and golfing, and a few catering to first-time homebuyers.

New growth was not accepted by all municipalities on the urban fringe, as many worked to actively protect their remaining natural resources. The region's

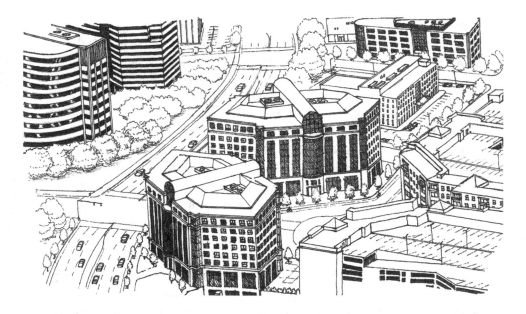

Figure 9.4 Edge city, 2000. By the new millennium the suburbs along the region's beltways sprouted massive office campuses, multistory malls, multiplexes, restaurants, structured parking garages, and even skyscrapers. These centers of activity, located ten, twenty, or even thirty miles from the traditional center, were truly edge cities.

land conservation movement drew from a number of roots. In part it mirrored the architectural preservation movement in the City itself with its desire to keep things as they had been. It hoped that by stopping change, property values of single-family homes might be preserved. In addition, undeveloped land, forest, field, and wetlands came to be understood as a series of environments that together served as a valuable resource for the region by lowering air temperature, filtering water, and maintaining a diverse store of birds, plants, and animals. This understanding was framed within an often nebulous notion of sustainability: an idea that urban development could not only coexist with nature, but learn from it and benefit from it by utilizing renewable energy, respecting natural systems, and pursuing various other strategies capable of reducing the human footprint. Beginning in the 1990s more and more land was bought up by state and local authorities for conservation and public use. Regional authorities also oversaw wetland restoration, improved treatment of sewage, runoff management,

Figures 9.5, 9.6 Shopping malls, 1975 and 2000. By 2000 shopping malls were frequently being designed to mimic the feel of traditional town centers, with neotraditional architecture and open-air walkways between stores replacing the enclosed spaces of the typical mall of previous decades.

and harbor cleanup efforts. State legislation introduced measures for the evaluation of development impacts on sensitive environmental resources, and to force the mitigation of those impacts found to be significant.[3]

Often the call was for conservation of the built character and existing social fabric of the suburb. Some towns resisted development by introducing larger minimum lot sizes, which inflated the prices of new housing and lowered the number of incoming families. Some towns balanced the desire for conservation and change by negotiating planned unit developments or adopting cluster zoning. These measures allowed developers to build on their parcels at higher densities than usually allowed, often employing town house configurations, but in return for leaving other parts of their parcels as open space or for other community benefits. Other towns' residents developed land trusts that successfully slowed the pace of development by buying up easements on forest or agricultural land.

Figure 9.7 Suburban development, 2000. Many of the suburban subdivisions of the later twentieth century were among the most expansive the City had ever seen, with broader streets to accommodate new regulations and larger lots to satisfy middle-class tastes. These homes, criticized as McMansions by some, were in some places so frantically built and so desperately sought after that they became ground zero for the subprime mortgage crisis in the early twenty-first century.

While these towns did achieve a stability not seen in adjacent areas, their exclusivity, not unlike that of gentrifying urban neighborhoods and wealthy inner suburbs, drove up regional housing costs and forced development ever outward. Reformers concerned with the consumption of resources asked if the demand for growth could be channeled into already developed areas under the auspices of "smart growth" policies. They put forward policies of denser residential development and tried to channel growth into areas served by public transit. These concerns, however, generally did not outweigh the willingness of many to pay for long commutes and higher taxes and to ignore environmental costs. Polycentrism and horizontal spread continued as the dominant geographic characteristics of the millennial decade.

THE PEOPLE OF THE GLOBAL CITY

The pace of social change begun in the 1960s with safe and inexpensive birth control measures and the revival of the feminist movement continued into the new millennium. Since the seventies women had entered the workforce in large numbers both to seek an independent life and to help support their families. They did so even though they earned only two-thirds as much as men for equivalent work. Two-parent families became a minority among the City's households. During the seventies and eighties this shift from a dominant pattern of early marriage and stay-at-home wives and mothers caused considerable family turmoil, but in time the well-to-do developed a stable marriage pattern. In the new adaptation, young professionals and business people tended to live together while postponing marriage. Then, supported by a good income, they married late, had small families, and suffered fewer divorces than the general population. This social pattern in turn drove up the City's real estate market for studio and one-bedroom apartments.

Most City dwellers, however, had yet to find a stable pattern in the process from youth to marriage. They were torn between the possibilities presented by the surrounding culture of sexual freedom and popular luxuries on the one hand, and on the other hand the strict discipline required by limited and uncertain incomes. They continued to marry early in life, but a high divorce rate and out-of-wedlock births challenged their efforts to maintain traditional ways.[4]

A variety of changes emerged to lead the old inner-city neighborhoods into a welcome pattern of some stability. New immigrant occupation of old areas, a new policing policy, and a number of municipal and private institutional efforts together stabilized the old streetcar neighborhoods. Starting in the 1970s after the United States lifted its quota system on foreign immigrants, economically declining areas of the inner city were reinvigorated by new immigrant groups—Latinos, South and Southeast Asians, Chinese, Koreans, Eastern Europeans, West and East Africans, West Indians, and Arabs leaving behind the civil and economic strife in their own countries. By 2000 the City featured new commercial districts in long-declining working-class areas, a Little Ethiopia and Little Saigon among others. In these districts neighborhood markets grew to serve a regional clientele. Historic Chinatown, Ukrainian, and Russian neighborhoods began to receive new immigrants in substantial numbers for the first time in decades. West Indians and Latinos settled throughout inner-city neighborhoods where gentrification had not taken over. New immigrants profited for themselves, their communities, and the home countries, where many of them maintained family ties and to which they often returned.

While business and residential districts experienced much new activity, they also saw interracial tensions not unlike those of a hundred years before. Those on the fringes of society but never far from the minds of many inner-city residents—the gangs—found new opponents. Though a peaceful mixture of new and old residents was generally the rule, some long-time residents despaired at the apparent success of new immigrant groups, even viewing it as a takeover as property began to shift into the hands of successful new-immigrant business owners. The City's traditional African American community was in fact declining in numbers by the end of the twentieth century, as more and more sought residence in nearby suburbs or in the opportunity-rich urban regions of the south.

A new police strategy succeeded in reducing crime rates in the 1990s. Police sought the help of residents in identifying gang-related violence. Officers were encouraged to develop personal relationships with residents and the community leaders of every group to gain their trust. This strategy, while achieving its stated goals to lower the number of guns and gang members on the streets, carried with it a costly self-defeating result: it packed the region's prisons.

The replacement of trouble-ridden high-rise housing projects with more pedestrian-scaled mixed-income neighborhoods under the federal Hope VI program also helped to keep the civic peace. However, it was local neighborhood action and a growing number of inner-city-focused nonprofit agencies that brought the most profound challenges to unemployment, undereducation, lending discrimination, and other problems of the inner city. Local health providers diversified their staff and services to confront health issues among a population that understood sickness and health in different languages and in different ways. Locally based community development corporations mounted political pressure on City Hall for more frequent garbage service and streetscape improvements, and communicated local trouble spots to police. They also pressured City Hall to pursue acquisition and disposition of vacant lots through eminent domain or tax foreclosure. Consequently many vacant properties were transformed into mixed-income housing development through public-private partnerships. As an urban environmental movement thrived, many of these lots found new lives as valued open space: as playgrounds and community gardens. In the context of the federal welfare reform movement of the 1990s, community groups, city government, and nonprofits created multiple welfare-to-work and adult education programs. The most effective of these channeled inner-city labor into the City's growing health and service sectors. Occasionally inner-city entrepreneurs were able to take advantage of outsourcing opportunities from large institutions; their stories sometimes made front page news in the regional papers. Charter schools offered a promising alternative to the City's troubled public school system.

Suburbanites composed a significantly more diverse lot by the new millennium. Inner suburbs that had once housed mostly white working-class commuters were in 2000 characterized by as much ethnic diversity as the City itself. Immigrants from all over the world—from East Asia, the Middle East, India, Africa, and Russia—remade the commercial districts of these old inner suburbs with their stores. Prosperous immigrants settled in the beltway communities distant from the City's center. Many enrolled in local schools and universities, eventually finding temporary or permanent employment in high-paying jobs after graduation. They added significantly to research and creativity in many fields, locally and in their places of origin.

The continued success of so many, however, immigrants and natives alike, faced a new threat. The health care, finance, research, and service economy had wonderfully benefited the top two-fifths of the population, but by the end of the twentieth century the costs of housing, transportation, child care, and education collided with the slow growth of wages and income among the middle class and working class. Many sought opportunities in other regions of the United States, especially the South and West. If not for the high level of international immigration, the region would have lost population.

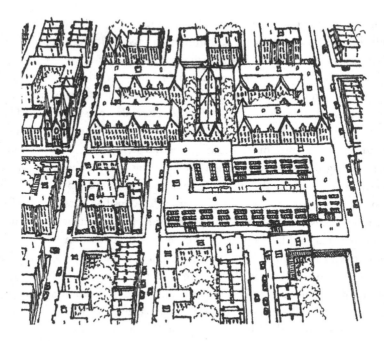

Figure 9.8   Hope VI project, 2000, a later view of the scene pictured on page 124. At the close of the twentieth century the federal government introduced the Hope VI program to replace failing public housing projects with mixed-income housing developments. These typically took on a neotraditional character, fitting into the scale of the surrounding neighborhood.

State intervention to promote affordable housing, funding for multiunit construction, and financial relief to towns did alleviate the situation somewhat, but for many residents the region simply could not compete. Banks and mortgage corporations exploited family financial stress by supplying subprime mortgages for properties across the region. They particularly focused on working-class urban areas and the most distant new middle-class suburbs, practices that came back to haunt them, their borrowers, and the communities a few years later.

From the downtown to the distant suburbs, the last decades of the twentieth century were times in which the conception of this City became ever more elusive to its own residents. Just as in the first historically unprecedented moments when the City's size had leapt to 500,000 and then 1,000,000, inhabitants of the City and its region knew their setting only through their specialized paths. Each individual went about his or her business increasingly unaware of the ever larger interdependent networks that each activity depended upon, from buying clothes to browsing online to cooking a meal. Most people would never know the names of more than a small percentage of people they encountered daily. The lifelong resident family grew ever more unusual.

It was a city, however, in which the people one did know most likely came from an increasing variety of backgrounds: almost all of the region's residents were more likely than their predecessors not to stay there, to have several jobs, not to have been born or raised there, and to live in several homes over time. People still knew each other from work, home, school, or religious institutions, but also from the Internet and from experience with several jobs. Often friends lived scattered through many towns and neighborhoods, and their children attended different schools. Friendships and acquaintances reached to people in other states and countries and any number of further social networks.

Such social dispersal had become ordinary. Few stopped to wonder how their predecessors had lived; if they did, they perhaps disliked the thought of having less convenience or fewer opportunities (however inaccurate such a historical perception might be). Even fewer thought to consider that there had previously been times of remarkable global change and instability, local inequality, and rapid changes in the economy and in opportunity. Theirs was not uniquely a time of change: change had always been the City's life and strength.

Notes

1 The City's Seventeenth-Century Beginnings

1. Stokes, 10.

2. Stokes, 13.

3. Stokes, 13.

4. Weil, 60.

5. Nash 1979, 16.

6. A mob in Boston threatened Governor Andros, who fled to the town's fort and later surrendered and was shipped back to England in chains. Vrabel, 35.

7. In the history of New York this breach in the social order is called "Leisler's Rebellion." Burrows and Wallace, 96–102.

2 The City in the Mid-Eighteenth Century

1. Small, narrow wooden row houses like these survived for a century or more in Philadelphia (Finkel, 10), and there are survivals of this kind on the north slope of Beacon Hill and in the South End of Boston.

2. Smith, 148.

3. Such a panic in the history of New York City besmirched its reputation as an open and tolerant city. See Lepore.

3 The Merchant Republic, 1820

1. See Kamensky.

2. Giovanni and Pietro Del-Monico: see Burrows and Wallace, 436–437.

3. Examples of the era were Beacon Hill, Boston, and the speculator Samuel B. Ruggles's Gramercy Park development in New York City.

4. Nash 2002, 145.

5. Burrows and Wallace, 546.

6. Burrows and Wallace, 483.

4 The City Overwhelmed, 1860

1. Griscom, 46–47.

2. *New York Times*, January 21, 1866.

3. Scobey, 117.

4. See the map of the New York 1863 riot in Burrows and Wallace, 891.

5 The City Restructured, 1895

1. The Belgian block is now commonly referred to by the name of its predecessor, the "cobblestone." The rectangular Belgian block was cut from New England granite with a flat face so that when set in sand on a concrete base it made a continuous and virtually indestructible surface. Such streets successfully resisted the wear of heavy iron-shod horses and steel-rimmed wagon wheels. In a few places end-grain wooden blocks set in sand on a concrete base and joined by pitch made a smooth, silent, but slippery surface for elegant neighborhoods. This treatment proved quite durable, unlike the notoriously fast-rotting Nicholson system. See McShane, chapter 4.

2. McShane and Tarr, 17.

3. Burrows and Wallace, 1061.

4. Douglas, 39–42; Willis, 8–9.

5. See Cahan.

6. Plunz, 22–28.

7. Veiller, 193–240.

8. See Fogel.

9. Burrows and Wallace, 1107.

10. See Riis; Weber, chapter 8.

11. Burt and Davies, 492.

12. Lane, 158, 17.

13. Hitchcock, 122–124, 132.

14. Burrows and Wallace, 1088.

6 Toward a New Economy and a Novel Urban Form, 1925

1. Lampard, 27.

2. Lampard, 24.

3. Zoning in New York City came about through an alliance between downtown property owners wary of skyscrapers and midtown retailers fearful of immigrant-employing garment factories. See Toll, chapters 2 and 3.

4. See Weiss, chapter 4.

5. Colean, 229.

6. See Weiss.

7. Grebler, Blank, and Winnick, 472–473; Willis, 162–164.

8. Loucks 1, 42.

9. Simpson, 163–171.

10. Hutchinson, 15. In what is sometimes called the "First Great Migration," the City's African American population grew disproportionately from 1895 to 1925, from 80,000 to 200,000.

11. Northern race riots: Springfield, Illinois, 1908, a false rumor of rape; Brooklyn, New York, movie patrons riot when an African American actor appears in a film with white ones; Chester, Pennsylvania, 1918, competition for housing, 5 killed; Philadelphia, same year and issue, 4 deaths; Chicago, 1919, competition for housing; Detroit, 1925, competition for housing; Carteret, New Jersey, 1926, rumor of a murder; Harlem, New York City, 1928, African Americans riot when a policeman tries to arrest an African American.

12. Hitchcock, 202–203.

7 THE FEDERALLY SUPPORTED CITY, 1950

1. According to the *Statistical Abstract of the United States* for 1930, p. 387, there were 4.9 million motor vehicles in the mid-Atlantic states of New York, Pennsylvania, and New Jersey, this figure including passenger automobiles and trucks, for 26.3 million people in those states. According to the *Statistical Abstract of the United States* for 1950, p. 489, there were 7.1 million motor vehicles for 29.9 million people in that region.

2. See Weingroff.

3. Fishman, 196–197.

4. Estimates based on Berry and Cohen, 439–440.

5. Hanchett, 164–165.

6. Hanchett, 166–171.

7. Weiss 1980, 53–59.

8. Weiss 1980, 53.

9. Greg Hise, in *Magnetic Los Angeles*, details how the United States Housing Authority explored homekeeping in the 1930s, erecting movable walls on tracks that could be adjusted as staged housekeepers went about cooking, washing, and cleaning. The American Public Health Association declared in 1934 that a home of 400 cubic feet per person should be a minimum standard. In 1936, the average new home receiving an FHA-insured mortgage had 5.8 rooms; in 1940 it had 5.1 rooms. Figures from Hise, 69.

10. "Residential development so extensive that it forms a remarkable chapter of its own in the history of Sothern California": *Los Angeles Times*, June 7, 1942, on the building of the Westchester district of Los Angeles.

11. This was the experience of Levitt and Sons in Levittown, New York.

12. Bergman and Bergman, 522.

13. Hirsch 2006.

14. Hirsch 2000.

8 The Polycentric City, 1975

1. See Weingroff.

2. Abrams, 8.

3. According to Paul E. Peterson in *The New Urban Reality*, in 1980 the population of Chicago's Robert Taylor Homes was 20,000, with an additional 5,000–7,000 unregistered adult residents. All of the registered households were black and 72 percent of residents were minors. In both the Robert Taylor Homes and Chicago's Cabrini Green, single women headed 90 percent of households with children; 81 percent of households with children in the Robert Taylor Homes and 70 percent of households with children in Cabrini Green received aid to families with dependent children (AFDC). In Cabrini Green 70 percent of all registered persons were on welfare. See Peterson, 137.

4. The postwar landscape of suburbanization is an oft-criticized cultural and physical feature of the modern United States. See Kenneth Jackson's *Crabgrass Frontier* (1987); James Kunstler's *Geography of Nowhere* (1994); or Jane Holtz Kay's *Asphalt Nation* (1998). For a rebuttal, see Robert Venturi's, *Learning from Las Vegas* (1977).

5. According to the *Statistical Abstract of the United States* for 1974, p. 547, the share of intercity freight transported by rail declined from 57.44 percent in 1950 to 37.77 percent in 1972. The share of freight transported by motor vehicle increased from 15.8 percent to 22.63 percent in the same period. That shipped by waterway rose from 14.93 percent to 16.31 percent, and that shipped by pipeline from 11.81 percent to 23.11 percent.

6. According to Jon Teaford in *City and Suburb*, between 1950 and 1970 the white population of New York City declined 7 percent and the black population rose 46 percent; in Chicago the white population dropped 13 percent while the black population rose 65 percent; in Philadelphia the white population dropped 13 percent and the black population rose 41 percent. See Teaford 1979, 115.

7. See *Linmark Associates v. Willingboro Township*, 431 U.S. 85 (1977). This case invalidated an ordinance designed to limit white flight by limiting "for sale" signs.

8. According to James Brady, in New York City 40,000 acts of arson were committed between 1975 and 1978. From 1951 to 1977 arson cases in the United States increased from only 5,600 to 177,000 annually.

9. Based on figures from the *Statistical Abstract of the United States* for 1976.

10. According to the Economic Policy Institute, the high school–college wage differential consistently shrank each year in this decade, from 37.7 percent in 1973 to 26.5 percent in 1979 for women and from 25.3 percent in 1973 to 20.5 percent in 1979 for men. (It has since risen to 47.1 percent for women and 43.1 percent for men in 2005.) Economic Policy Institute, "Estimated Wage Premium for College and High School Graduates, 1973–2005," <http://www.epi.org/datazone/06/college_premium.xls>, accessed August 16, 2010.

9 THE GLOBAL CITY, 2000

1. According to the Economic Policy Institute's "The State of Working America 2006–2007," between 1979 and 2000 the real income of households in the lowest fifth grew by 6.1 percent, that of the middle fifth by 12.3 percent, and that of the top fifth by 70 percent. The real income of the top 1 percent of households grew by 184 percent. Mischel et al., 40.

2. Fulton et al. found that while the metropolitan population of the United States grew by 17 percent between 1982 and 1997, the area of urbanized land within these metropolitan areas grew by 47 percent. The authors state that metropolitan density declined from 5.0 persons per urbanized acre in 1982 to 4.22 in 1997.

3. See for example the California Environmental Quality Act (CEQA), California Public Resources Code §21000 et seq., enacted in 1970.

4. The differential marriage patterns are discussed in Cahn and Carbone.

Suggested Reading

Introduction

Looking

Appleyard, Donald, Kevin Lynch, and John R. Myer. *The View from the Road*. Cambridge, MA: MIT Press, 1964.

Clay, Grady. *Close Up: How to Read the American City*. New York: Praeger, 1973.

Cullen, Gordon. *Townscape*. New York: Reinhold, 1961.

Gehl, Jan. *Life between Buildings: Using Public Space*. New York: Van Nostrand Reinhold, 1987.

Jacobs, Allan B. *Looking at Cities*. Cambridge, MA: Harvard University Press, 1965.

Jacobs, Jane. *The Death and Life of Great American Cities*. New York: Random House, 1961.

Lynch, Kevin. *The Image of the City*. Cambridge, MA: MIT Press, 1960.

Whyte, William H. *The Social Life of Small Urban Spaces*. Washington, DC: Conservation Foundation, 1980.

Transportation

Chinitz, Benjamin. *Freight and the Metropolis*. Cambridge, MA: Harvard University Press, 1960.

Downs, Anthony. *Stuck in Traffic: Coping with Peak-Hour Traffic Congestion*. Washington, DC: Brookings Institution, 1992.

Garreau, Joel. *Edge Cities: Life on the New Frontier*. New York: Doubleday, 1991.

Southworth, Michael, and Eran Ben-Joseph. *Streets and the Shaping of Towns and Cities*. Washington, DC: Island Press, 2003.

Vance, James E. *The North American Railroad: Its Origin, Evolution, and Geography*. Baltimore: Johns Hopkins University Press, 1995.

Warner, Sam Bass. *Streetcar Suburbs: The Process of Growth in Boston, 1870–1900*. Cambridge, MA: Harvard University Press, 1962.

Real Estate, Land Economics

Alonso, William. *Location and Land Use*. Cambridge, MA: Harvard University Press, 1964.

Clark, Colin. *Population Growth and Land Use*. London: Macmillan, 1967.

George, Henry. *Progress and Poverty*. 1879; reprint, New York: Robert Schalkenbach Foundation, 1979.

Hoyt, Homer. *One Hundred Years of Land Values in Chicago: The Relationship of the Growth of Chicago to the Rise in Its Land Values, 1830–1933*. Chicago: University of Chicago Press, 1933.

Hurd, Richard M. *Principles of City Land Values*. 1903; reprint, New York: Record & Guide, 1924.

Jacobs, Jane. *Cities and the Wealth of Nations: Principles of Economic Life*. New York: Random House, 1984.

Perrin, Constance. *Everything in Its Place: Social Order and Land Use in America*. Princeton: Princeton University Press, 1977.

Toll, Seymour I. *Zoned American*. New York: Grossman Publishers, 1969.

Who Lives Where? Urban Sociology

Addams, Jane, et al. *Hull House Maps and Papers*. New York: T. Y. Crowell, 1895.

Drake, St. Clair, and Horace R. Cayton. *Black Metropolis: A Study of Negro Life in a Northern City*. New York: Harcourt Brace, 1945.

Frug, Gerald. *City Making: Building Community without Building Walls*. Princeton: Princeton University Press, 1999.

Isenberg, Allison. *Downtown America: A History of the Place and the People Who Made It*. Chicago: Chicago University Press, 2004.

Kain, John F., and Joseph J. Persky. "The Ghetto, the Metropolis and the Nation." Discussion Paper, Harvard University Program on Regional and Urban Economics, no. 30. Cambridge, MA: Harvard University, 1968.

Logan, John R., and Harvey L. Molotch. *Urban Fortunes: The Political Economy of Place*. Berkeley: University of California Press, 2007.

Orfield, Myron. *Metropolitics: A Regional Agenda for Community and Stability*. Washington, DC: Brookings Institute and Lincoln Institute of Land Policy, 1997.

Park, Robert Ezra, Ernest W. Burgess, Roderick D. McKenzie, with a bibliography by Louis Wirth. *The City*. Chicago: University of Chicago Press, 1925.

Ward, David. *Poverty, Ethnicity and the American City, 1840–1925: Changing Conceptions of the Slum and the Ghetto*. New York: Cambridge University Press, 1989.

Woods, Robert A., and Albert J. Kennedy. *The Zone of Emergence: Observations of the Lower Middle and Upper Working Class Communities of Boston, 1905–1914.* 2nd ed. Cambridge, MA: Harvard University Press, 1969.

Zorbaugh, Harvey. *Gold Coast and Slum: A Sociological Study of Chicago's New North Side.* Chicago: University of Chicago Press, 1929.

General

Bennett, Ralph, ed. *Settlements in the Americas: Cross Cultural Perspectives.* Newark: University of Delaware Press, 1993.

Ciucci, Giorgio, et al. *The American City: From the Civil War to the New Deal.* Cambridge, MA: MIT Press, 1979.

Fishman, Robert. *Bourgeois Utopias: The Rise and Fall of Suburbia.* New York: Basic Books, 1989.

Mumford, Lewis. *The Culture of Cities.* New York: Harcourt Brace, 1938.

Reps, John. *The Making of Urban America: A History of City Planning in the United States.* Princeton: Princeton University Press, 1965.

Vernon, Raymond. *Metropolis 1985.* Cambridge, MA: Harvard University Press, 1960.

Warner, Sam Bass. *Greater Boston: Adapting Regional Traditions to the Present.* Philadelphia: University of Pennsylvania Press, 2001.

I   THE CITY'S SEVENTEENTH-CENTURY BEGINNINGS

Burrows, Edwin G., and Mike Wallace. *Gotham: A History of New York City to 1898.* New York: Oxford University Press, 1999.

Ceci, Lynn. *The Effect of European Contact and Trade on Settlement Patterns of Indians in Coastal New York, 1524–1665.* New York: Garland, 1990.

Dunn, Mary Maples, and Richard S. Dunn. "The Founding, 1681–1701." In *Philadelphia: A 300-Year History,* ed. Russell F. Weigley, 1–44. New York: W. W. Norton, 1982.

Foster, Stephen. "The Godly Transit: English Popular Protestantism and the Creation of a Puritan Establishment in America." In *Seventeenth-Century New England: A Conference Held by the Colonial Society of Massachusetts, June 18 and 19, 1982,* 185–238. Boston: Colonial Society of Massachusetts, 1984.

Grumet, Robert S. *Historic Contact: Indian People and Colonists in Today's Northeastern United States in the Sixteenth through Eighteenth Centuries.* Norman, OK: University of Oklahoma Press, 1995.

Henretta, James A. "Economic Development and Social Structure in Colonial Boston." In *Colonial America: Essays in Politics and Social Development*, ed. Stanley Katz, 359–374. Boston: Little, Brown, 1976.

Nash, Gary B. *First City: Philadelphia and the Forging of Historical Meaning*. Philadelphia: University of Pennsylvania Press, 2002.

Nash, Gary B. *The Urban Crucible*. Cambridge, MA: Harvard University Press, 1979.

Schlesinger, Arthur Meier. *The Rise of the City, 1878–1898*. New York: Macmillan, 1933.

Stokes, Isaac Newton Phelps. *Iconography of Manhattan Island, 1498–1909*. Vol. 1. 1915; reprint, New York: Arno Press, 1967.

Vrabel, Jim. *When in Boston: A Time Line and Almanac*. Boston: Northeastern University Press, 2004.

Weil, François. *A History of New York*. Trans. Jody Gladding. New York: Columbia University Press, 2004.

2 The City in the Mid-Eighteenth Century

Blackmar, Elizabeth. *Manhattan for Rent, 1785–1850*. Ithaca: Cornell University Press, 1989.

Finkel, Kenneth. *Philadelphia Then and Now*. Philadelphia: Library Company of Philadelphia, 1968.

Lepore, Jill. *New York Burning*. New York: Knopf, 2005.

Nash, Gary B. *The Urban Crucible*. Cambridge, MA: Harvard University Press, 1979.

Smith, Billy G. *The "Lower Sort": Philadelphia's Laboring People, 1750–1800*. Ithaca: Cornell University Press, 1990.

Weil, François. *A History of New York*. Trans. Jody Gladding. New York: Columbia University Press, 2004.

3 The Merchant Republic, 1820

Blackmar, Elizabeth. *Manhattan for Rent, 1785–1850*. Ithaca: Cornell University Press, 1989.

Burrows, Edwin G., and Mike Wallace. *Gotham: A History of New York City to 1898*. New York: Oxford University Press, 1999.

Kamensky, Jane. *The Exchange Artist*. New York: Viking Penguin, 2008.

Montgomery, David. "The Working Classes of the Pre-Industrial American City, 1780–1830." *Labor History* 42 (2001): 3–22.

Nash, Gary B. *First City: Philadelphia and the Forging of Historical Memory*. Philadelphia: University of Pennsylvania Press, 2002.

Nash, Gary B. *Forging Freedom: The Formation of Philadelphia's Black Community, 1720–1840*. Cambridge, MA: Harvard University Press, 1988.

Reps, John W. *The Making of Urban America: A History of City Planning in the United States*. Princeton: Princeton University Press, 1965.

Scherzer, Kenneth A. *The Unbounded Community: Neighborhood Life and Social Structure in New York City, 1830–1875*. Durham: Duke University Press, 1992.

Stokes, Isaac Newton Phelps. *Iconography of Manhattan Island, 1498–1909*. Vols. 1 and 3. 1915; reprint, New York: Arno Press, 1967

Vance, James E., Jr. "Land Assignment in the Precapitalist, Capitalist and Postcapitalist City." *Economic Geography* 47 (1971): 101–120.

Vrabel, Jim. *When in Boston: A Time Line and Almanac*. Boston: Northeastern University Press, 2004.

4 THE CITY OVERWHELMED, 1860

Burrows, Edwin G., and Mike Wallace. *Gotham: A History of New York City to 1898*. New York: Oxford University Press, 1999.

Domosh, Mona. *Invented Cities: The Creation of Landscape in Nineteenth-Century New York and Boston*. New Haven: Yale University Press, 1996.

Geffen, Elizabeth M. "Industrial Development and Social Crisis, 1841–1854." In *Philadelphia: A 300-Year History*, ed. Russell F. Weigley, 307–362. New York: W. W. Norton, 1982.

Griscom, John H. *The Sanitary Condition of the Laboring Population of New York with Suggestions for Its Improvement*. 1848; reprint, New York: Harper Brothers, Arno Press, 1970.

Handlin, Oscar. *Boston's Immigrants*. 2nd ed. Cambridge, MA: Harvard University Press, 1979.

Lane, Roger. *Policing the City: Boston, 1825–1885*. Cambridge, MA: Harvard University Press, 1967.

Lockwood, Charles. *Bricks and Brownstone: The New York Row House, 1783–1929*. New York: McGraw Hill, 1972.

Nash, Gary B. *First City: Philadelphia and the Forging of Historical Meaning*. Philadelphia: University of Pennsylvania Press, 2002.

Plunz, Richard. *A History of Housing in New York City: Dwelling Types and Social Change in the American Metropolis*. New York: Columbia University Press, 1990.

Scherzer, Kenneth A. *The Unbounded Community: Neighborhood Life and Social Structure in New York City, 1830–1875*. Durham: Duke University Press, 1992.

Scobey, David M. *Empire City: The Making and Meaning of the New York City Landscape*. Philadelphia: Temple University Press, 2002.

Stansell, Christine. *City of Women: Sex and Class in New York, 1789–1860*. New York: Alfred A. Knopf, 1986.

Warner, Sam Bass. *The Private City: Philadelphia in Three Periods of Its Growth*. 2nd ed. Philadelphia: University of Pennsylvania Press, 1987.

Wiebe, Robert H. *Self-Rule: A Cultural History of American Democracy*. Chicago: University of Chicago Press, 1995.

5   THE CITY RESTRUCTURED, 1895

Burrows, Edwin G., and Mike Wallace. *Gotham: A History of New York City to 1898*. New York: Oxford University Press, 1999.

Burt, Nathaniel, and Wallace E. Davies. "The Iron Age, 1876–1905." In *Philadelphia: A 300-Year History*, ed. Russell F. Weigley, 471–523. New York: W. W. Norton, 1982.

Cahan, Abraham. *The Rise of David Levinsky. 1917; reprint*. New York: Harper and Row, 1960.

Chandler, Alfred D. *The Visible Hand: The Managerial Revolution in American Business*. Cambridge, MA: Harvard University Press, 1977.

Cheape, Charles W. *Moving the Masses: Urban Public Transit in New York, Boston, and Philadelphia, 1880–1912*. Cambridge, MA: Harvard University Press, 1980.

Douglas, George H. *Skyscrapers: A Social History of the Very Tall Building in America*. Jefferson, NC: McFarland, 1996.

Fogel, Robert William. "The Conquest of High Mortality and Hunger in Europe and America." NBER Working Paper Series on Historical Factors in Long Run Rates of Growth, Historical Paper #16. National Bureau of Economic Research, 1990.

Fogelson, Robert M. *Downtown: Its Rise and Fall, 1880–1950*. New Haven: Yale University Press, 2001.

Hitchcock, H. Wiley. *Music in the United States*. Englewood Cliffs, NJ: Prentice Hall, 1988.

Lane, Roger. *The Roots of Violence in Black Philadelphia, 1860–1900*. Cambridge, MA: Harvard University Press, 1986.

Lane, Roger. *William Dorsey's Philadelphia and Ours.* New York: Oxford University Press, 1991.

McShane, Clay. *Down the Asphalt Path: The Automobile and the American City.* New York: Columbia University Press, 1994.

McShane, Clay, and Joel A. Tarr. *The Horse in the City.* Baltimore: Johns Hopkins University Press, 2007.

Montgomery, David. *The Fall of the House of Labor: The Workplace, the State, and American Labor Activism, 1865–1925.* New Haven: Yale University Press, 1989.

O'Connor, Thomas H. *The Hub: Boston Past and Present.* Boston: Northeastern University Press, 2001.

Plunz, Richard. *A History of Housing in New York City: Dwelling Types and Social Change in the American Metropolis.* New York: Columbia University Press, 1990.

Riis, Jacob A. *How the Other Half Lives.* 1890; reprint, ed. Sam Bass Warner, Cambridge, MA: Harvard University Press, 1970.

Veiller, Lawrence. "A Statistical Study of New York's Tenement Houses." In *The Tenement House Problem*, ed. Robert W. De Forest and Lawrence Veiller, 2 vols., 1:193–240. 1903; reprint, New York: Arno Press, 1970.

Weber, Adna Ferin. *The Growth of Cities in the Nineteenth Century: A Study in Statistics.* 1899; reprint, Ithaca: Cornell University Press, 1963.

Willis, Carol. *Form Follows Finance: Skyscrapers and Skylines in New York and Chicago.* New York: Princeton Architectural Press, 2003.

6   Toward a New Economy and a Novel Urban Form, 1925

Cheape, Charles N. *Moving the Masses: Public Transit in New York, Boston, and Philadelphia, 1880–1912.* Cambridge, MA: Harvard University Press, 1980.

Colean, Miles. *American Housing: Problems and Prospects.* New York: Twentieth Century Fund, 1944.

Fogelson, Robert M. *Bourgeois Nightmares: Suburbia, 1870–1930.* New Haven: Yale University Press, 2005.

Fogelson, Robert M. *Downtown: Its Rise and Fall, 1880–1950.* New Haven: Yale University Press, 2001.

Grebler, Leo, David M. Blank, and Louis Winnick. *Capital Formation in Residential Real Estate.* Princeton: Princeton University Press, 1956.

Hitchcock, H. Wiley. *Music in the United States.* Englewood Cliffs, NJ: Prentice Hall, 1988.

Hutchinson, George. *The Cambridge Companion to the Harlem Renaissance*. New York: Cambridge University Press, 2007.

Lampard, Eric E. Introductory Essay. In *Inventing Times Square*, ed. William R. Taylor. New York: Russell Sage Foundation, 1991.

Loucks, William N. *The Philadelphia Plan of Home Financing*. Chicago: Institute for Research in Land Economics and Public Utilities, 1929.

McShane, Clay. *Down the Asphalt Path: The Automobile and the American City*. New York: Columbia University Press, 1994.

Montgomery, David. *The Fall of the House of Labor: The Workplace, the State, and American Labor Activism, 1865–1925*. New Haven: Yale University Press, 1989.

Simpson, Herbert D. "Real Estate Speculation and the Depression." *American Economic Review* 23 (March 1933): 163–171.

Sussman, Carl, ed. *Planning the Fourth Migration: The Neglected Vision of the Regional Planning Association of America*. Cambridge, MA: MIT Press, 1976.

Taylor, William R., ed. *Inventing Times Square*. New York: Russell Sage Foundation, 1991.

Toll, Seymour I. *Zoned American*. New York: Grossman Publishers, 1969.

Weiss, Marc A. *The Rise of the Community Builders*. New York: Columbia University Press, 1987.

Willis, Carol. *Form Follows Finance: Skyscrapers and Skylines in New York and Chicago*. New York: Princeton Architectural Press, 2003.

7   THE FEDERALLY SUPPORTED CITY, 1950

Bergman, Peter M. with Mort N. Bergman. *The Chronological History of the Negro in America*. New York: Harper and Row, 1969.

Berry, Brian J., and Yehoshua S. Cohen. "Decentralization of Commerce and Industry: The Restructuring of Metropolitan America." In *The Urbanization of the Suburbs*, ed. Louis H. Masotti and Jeffrey K. Hadden. Urban Affairs Annual Reviews, 7. Beverly Hills: Sage Publications, 1973.

Caro, Robert. *The Power Broker: Robert Moses and the Fall of New York*. New York: Vintage, 1975.

Ewen, Elizabeth. *Picture Windows: How the Suburbs Happened*. New York: Basic Books, 2001.

Fishman, Robert. *Bourgeois Utopias: The Rise and Fall of Suburbia*. New York: Basic Books, 1987.

Gans, Herbert. *The Levittowners*. New York: Columbia University Press, 1982.

Greenburg, Cheryl Lynn. *"Or Does It Explode?" Black Harlem in the Great Depression*. New York: Oxford University Press, 1997.

Hall, Peter. *Cities of Tomorrow: An Intellectual History of Planning and Design in the Twentieth Century*. 3rd ed. Hoboken: Wiley-Blackwell, 2002.

Hanchett, Thomas W. "The Other Subsidized Housing: Federal Aid to Suburbanization 1940s–1960." In *From Tenements to the Taylor Homes: In Search of an Urban Housing Policy in Twentieth-Century America*, ed. John F. Bauman, Roger Biles, and Kristin M. Szylvian, 163–171. University Park: Pennsylvania State University Press, 2000.

Hirsch, Arnold R. "Choosing Segregation: Federal Policy between Shelley and Brown." In *From Tenements to the Taylor Homes: In Search of an Urban Housing Policy in Twentieth-Century America*, ed. John F. Bauman, Roger Biles, and Kristin M. Szylvian, 206–225. University Park: Pennsylvania State University Press, 2000.

Hirsch, Arnold R. "Less Than *Plessy*: The Inner City, Suburbs, and State-Sanctioned Residential Segregation in the Age of *Brown*." In *The New Suburban History*, ed. Kevin M. Kruse and Thomas J. Sugrue, 33–56. Chicago: University of Chicago Press, 2006.

Hise, Greg. *Magnetic Los Angeles: Planning the Twentieth Century Metropolis*. Baltimore: Johns Hopkins University Press, 1999.

Hoover, Edgar M., and Raymond Vernon. "The Anatomy of a Metropolis: The Changing Distribution of People and Jobs within the New York Metropolitan Region." Vol. 1 in *New York Metropolitan Region Study*. Garden City, NY: Doubleday, 1959.

Jackson, Kenneth. *Crabgrass Frontier: The Suburbanization of the United States*. New York: Oxford University Press, 1987.

Le Corbusier. *Towards a New Architecture*. Mineola, NY: Dover Publications, 1985.

Lehmann, Nicholas. *The Promised Land: The Great Black Migration and How It Changed America*. New York: Vintage Books, 1992.

McElvaine, Robert S. *The Great Depression: America, 1929–1941*. New York: Three Rivers Press, 1993.

Teaford, Jon C. *City and Suburb: The Political Fragmentation of Metropolitan America, 1850–1970*. Baltimore: Johns Hopkins University Press, 1979.

Vale, Lawrence J. *From the Puritans to the Projects: Public Housing and Public Neighbors*. Cambridge, MA: Harvard University Press, 2007.

Weingroff, Richard F. *Federal-Aid Highway Act of 1956: Creating the Interstate System*. Washington, DC: U.S. Department of Transportation, Federal Highway Administration, 2009.

Weiss, Marc A. "The Origins and Legacy of Urban Renewal." In *Urban and Regional Planning in an Age of Austerity*, ed. Pierre Clavel, John Forester, and William Goldsmith. New York: Pergamon, 1980.

8 THE POLYCENTRIC CITY, 1975

Abrams, Charles. *The Role and Responsibility of the Federal Highway System in Baltimore.* Baltimore: Johns Hopkins University Press, 1968.

Biles, Roger. "Public Housing and the Postwar Urban Rennaissance." In *From Tenements to the Taylor Homes: In Search of an Urban Housing Policy in Twentieth-Century America,* ed. John F. Bauman, Roger Biles, and Kristin M. Szylvian, 143–162. University Park: Pennsylvania State University Press, 2000.

Brady, James. "Arson, Urban Economy and Organized Crime: The Case of Boston." *Social Problems* 31 (1983): 1–27.

Cohen, Lizabeth. *A Consumer's Republic: The Politics of Mass Consumption in Postwar America.* New York: Vintage, 2003.

Coontz, Stephanie. *The Way We Never Were: American Families and the Nostalgia Trap.* New York: Basic Books, 2000.

Fisher, Robert. *Let the People Decide: Community Organizing in America.* Woodbridge, CT: Twayne Publishers, 1994.

Jackson, Kenneth. *Crabgrass Frontier: The Suburbanization of the United States.* New York: Oxford University Press, 1987.

Jacobs, Jane. *The Death and Life of Great American Cities.* New York: Random House, 1961.

Kay, Jane Holtz. *Asphalt Nation: How the Automobile Took Over America and How We Can Take It Back.* Berkeley: University of California Press, 1998.

Kunstler, James Howard. *The Geography of Nowhere: The Rise and Decline of America's Man-Made Landscape.* New York: Free Press, 1994.

Logan, John R., and Harvey L. Molotch. *Urban Fortunes: The Political Economy of Place.* 2nd ed. Berkeley: University of California Press, 2001.

Lukas, J. Anthony. *Common Ground: A Turbulent Decade in the Lives of Three American Families.* New York: Vintage Books, 1986.

Mohl, Raymond A., and Arnold R. Hirsch, eds. *Urban Policy in Twentieth-Century America.* New Brunswick: Rutgers University Press, 1993.

Mollenkopf, John H. *The Contested City.* Princeton: Princeton University Press, 1983.

Nicolaides, Becky M. *My Blue Heaven: Life and Politics in the Working-Class Suburbs of Los Angeles, 1920–1965.* Chicago: University of Chicago Press, 2002.

Peterson, Paul E., ed. *The New Urban Reality.* Washington, DC: Brookings Institution, 1985.

Rae, Douglas W. *City: Urbanism and Its End*. New Haven: Yale University Press, 2003.

Self, Robert O. *American Babylon: Race and the Struggle for Postwar Oakland*. 2005. Princeton: Princeton University Press.

Sugrue, Thomas J. *Race and Inequality in Postwar Detroit*. Princeton: Princeton University Press, 2005.

Teaford, Jon C. *City and Suburb: The Political Fragmentation of Metropolitan America, 1850–1970*. Baltimore: Johns Hopkins University Press, 1979.

Teaford, Jon C. *The Twentieth-Century American City: Problem, Promise, and Reality*. Baltimore: Johns Hopkins University Press, 1993.

Venturi, Robert. *Learning from Las Vegas: The Forgotten Symbolism of Architectural Form*. Cambridge, MA: MIT Press, 1977.

Waldie, D. J. *Holy Land: A Suburban Memoir*. New York: W. W. Norton, 2005.

Weingroff, Richard F. *Federal-Aid Highway Act of 1956: Creating the Interstate System*. Washington, DC: U.S. Department of Transportation, Federal Highway Administration, 2009.

Wilson, William Julius. *The Declining Significance of Race: Blacks and Changing American Institutions*. Chicago: University of Chicago Press, 1980.

9   THE GLOBAL CITY, 2000

Abu-Lughod, Janet. *New York, Chicago, Los Angeles: America's Global Cities*. Minneapolis: University of Minnesota Press, 2000.

Blakely, Edward J. *Fortress America: Gated Communities in the United States*. Washington, DC: Brookings Institution Press, 1999.

Cahn, Naomi, and Jane Carbone. *Red Families v. Blue Families: Legal Polarization and the Creation of Culture*. New York: Oxford University Press, 2010.

Davis, Mike. *City of Quartz: Excavating the Future in Los Angeles*. New York: Vintage, 1992.

Davis, Mike. *Magical Urbanism: Latinos Reinvent the US Big City*. London: Verso, 2001.

Dreier, Peter, et al. *Place Matters: Metropolitics for the Twenty-First Century*. Lawrence: University of Kansas Press, 2005.

Fishman, Robert. *Bourgeois Utopias: The Rise and Fall of Suburbia*. New York: Basic Books, 1989.

Frieden, Bernard J., and Lynne B. Sagalyn. *Downtown, Inc: How America Rebuilds Its Cities*. Cambridge, MA: MIT Press, 1989.

Fulton, William, et al. *Who Sprawls Most? How Growth Patterns Differ across the United States*. Washington, DC: Brookings Institution, 2001.

Garreau, Joel. *Edge City: Life on the New Frontier*. Norwell, MA: Anchor Press, 1992.

Grogan, Paul, and Tony Proscio. *Comeback Cities: A Blueprint for Neighborhood Revival*. New York: Basic Books, 2001.

Hayden, Dolores. *The Power of Place: Urban Landscapes as Public History*. Cambridge, MA: MIT Press, 1997.

Katz, Michael B. *The Undeserving Poor: From the War on Poverty to the War on Welfare*. New York: Pantheon, 1990.

Kay, Jane Holtz. *Asphalt Nation: How the Automobile Took Over America and How We Can Take It Back*. Berkeley: University of California Press, 1998.

Lee, Chang-Rae. *Aloft*. New York: Putnam, 2004.

Marcuse, Peter, and Ronald van Kempen. *Globalizing Cities: A New Spatial Order?* Hoboken: Wiley-Blackwell, 2000.

Massey, Douglas, and Nancy Denton. *American Apartheid: Segregation and the Making of the Underclass*. Cambridge, MA: Harvard University Press, 1998.

Mischel, Lawrence, et al. *The State of Working America 2006/2007*. Ithaca: Cornell University, 2007.

Orfield, Myron. *American Metropolitics: New Suburban Reality*. Washington, DC: Brookings Institution Press, 2002.

Rome, Adam. *The Bulldozer in the Countryside: Suburban Sprawl and the Rise of American Environmentalism*. Cambridge: Cambridge University Press, 2001.

Rybczynski, Witold. *City Life: Urban Expectations in a New World*. New York: Scribner, 1996.

Sassen, Saskia. *The Global City: New York, London, Tokyo*. Princeton: Princeton University Press, 2001.

Sorkin, Michael. *Variations on a Theme Park: The New American City and the End of Public Space*. New York: Hill and Wang, 1992.

Storper, Michael. *The Regional World: Territorial Development in a Global Economy*. New York: Guilford Press, 1997.

Wilson, William Julius. *There Goes the Neighborhood: Racial, Ethnic and Class Tensions in Four Chicago Neighborhoods and Their Meaning for America*. New York: Vintage, 2007.

Index

Abrams, Charles, 121
Advertising, 86, 107
African-Americans, 11, 13, 15, 28, 39, 42–43, 60, 77–80, 85, 97–98, 108, 113–114, 119–121, 128–131, 142, 150
  civic organizations, 43, 129
  civil rights, 114, 119–121, 128–130
  culture, 78–79, 97–98, 141
  and education, 43, 114, 129–130
  housing, 108, 114, 121, 128–129, 131
  migrations, 113, 119, 128
  and riots, 97, 113
  segregation, 39, 77, 108, 128–129
  and slavery, 11, 13, 15, 28
Agriculture, 9, 11, 21, 49–50, 96, 128
  of Amerindians, 9, 11
  of European colonists, 13, 21
  nineteenth-century, 49
  twentieth-century, 96, 128
Air conditioning, 126–127
Air pollution, 142
Airports, 127, 139
American Civil War, 53, 60, 77
American Express, 114
American Revolution, 33, 41, 43
Amerindians, 9–12, 21, 28, 33
  agriculture, 9, 11
  and epidemics, 10
  massacres of, 28
  products of, 9, 12
  relations with, 10, 33
  settlements, 9–10
  and trade, 9
  war with, 10, 33

Amsterdam, 14
Amusement parks, 74
Anglicans, 25
Annexation, 76
Architecture, 23, 35, 56, 94, 111, 122, 138, 140, 142, 146
  of colonial City, 23
  in nineteenth-century City, 35
  preservation of, 140, 142, 146
  of public housing, 122
  of suburbs, 56, 94, 111, 125
  of urban renewal, 122–123
Astor, John Jacob, 34
Automobiles, 86–87, 93, 104, 110, 121, 127, 142, 144

Baltimore, 121
Banking, 33–34, 87, 95, 108, 114, 128–129, 151–152. *See also* Finance
  discriminatory lending practices, 108, 128–129, 151
Bell, Alexander Graham, 69
Big-box stores, 107, 144–145
Birth control, 149
Blight, 111, 121
Blockbusting, 129
Blue Cross and Blue Shield, 114
Boston, 1–2, 67
Brazil, 14
Broadcasting. *See* Radio
Brown v. Board of Education, Topeka, Kansas, 114
Buses, 4, 121, 142
Business improvement districts, 143

Cadiz, 14
California, 49, 77, 125
Cambridge (Massachusetts), 14
Canals, 33, 43
Caribbean. *See* West Indies
Catholicism, 11, 59–60, 74, 78, 128
Charity, 28, 44, 139
Chicago, 2
Children, 24, 28, 42–44, 73, 140
    in colonial City, 24, 28
    and labor, 44, 73
    in nineteenth-century City, 42–43
    in twentieth-century City, 140
China, 71, 103
Chinatown, 122, 150
City planning, 91, 93, 110–111
Civic organizations, 43, 58, 97, 129
    of African-Americans, 43, 129
    of European immigrants, 58, 97
Class relations, 15, 17, 22, 27–29, 37, 39,
        42–44, 56, 59–61, 77, 87, 108, 111,
        114, 121, 128, 137
    in colonial City, 15, 17, 22, 27–29
    in nineteenth-century City, 37, 39,
        42–44, 56, 59–61
    and segregation, 39, 77, 87, 108, 111
    in twentieth-century City, 114, 121,
        128, 137
Clean Air Act, 127
Clean Water Act, 127
Coffeehouses, 27
Cold War, 103
Communism, 103–104
Community development corporations,
    151
Commuting, 3, 35, 50, 58, 66, 69, 77, 80,
        90, 112, 127, 145, 151
    by automobile, 127, 145
    by foot, 35, 50, 58
    by rail, 50, 69, 90, 112
    by streetcar, 66, 69
Computers, 138
Condominiums, 140

Construction methods, 14, 35, 53, 76, 112
    colonial regulation of, 14
    in nineteenth century, 35, 53, 76
    of postwar suburbs, 111
    and prefabrication, 111
Consumerism, 86, 96, 131
Corporations, 11, 65, 69, 74, 86–87, 90,
        114, 138, 142–143, 145, 152
Cotton, 33, 60, 113
Covenants. *See* Restrictive covenants
Craftsmen. *See* Tradesmen
Credit cards, 114
Crime, 16, 22, 43, 56, 59–60, 78, 129,
        131, 150–151
Cullen, Gordon, 3
Currency, 33

Darwin, Charles, 78
Defense industries, 111, 125
Democracy, 5, 29, 44, 59
Democratic party, 128
Department stores, 70, 86, 107, 126, 140
Depression. *See* Economic depression
Detroit, 113
Diners Club, 114
Docks. *See* Port facilities
Domestic life, 24–25, 28, 37, 44, 131, 149
    of colonial City, 24–25, 28
    of nineteenth-century City, 37
    of suburbanites, 131
Domestic occupations, 24, 43, 49, 58
Downtown, 53, 56, 58, 65–67, 69–71, 74,
        86–87, 89–91, 104, 107, 110, 120–
        122, 126–128, 139–140, 142–144
    decline, 104, 107, 110, 120–121, 126
    employment in, 107
    housing, 140
    office space, 90, 143
    retail, 53, 56, 65, 69–70, 86–87, 107,
        140, 142–143
    revival, 139–140
    urban renewal, 122–123, 139
Drugs. *See* Illegal drug use

Economic depression, 58, 60, 71, 73, 96,
    104, 110
    of 1837–1842, 58
    of 1857, 60
    of 1873, 71, 73
    of 1930s, 96, 104, 107, 110
Economic recession, 131, 138
    of 1970s, 131, 138
    of 1980s, 138
Edge cities, 145
Education, 14, 25–26, 39, 41–44, 78, 80,
    97, 113–114, 125, 130, 132, 137–139,
    144, 151. *See also* Higher education;
    Public education
    and African-Americans, 43, 114,
    129–130
    charter schools, 151
    in crafts, 39, 41
    and desegregation, 114, 129–130
    parochial schools, 78, 97, 130
Eisenhower, Dwight D., 104, 114
Electricity, 52, 66, 74, 87
Elevated railroads, 67, 69
Eliot, John, 10
England, 10, 16–17, 49, 58, 111
    housing programs in, 111
    immigration from, 16, 49, 58
Enlightenment, 14
Environmentalism, 127, 146–147, 151
Environmental Protection Agency, 127
Erie Canal, 43
Europe, 10–11, 14, 16–17, 24–25, 44, 49,
    61, 87
    immigration from, 16, 25, 49, 87
    investment from, 49
    religious wars, 10, 14, 16–17, 25
    revolution, 61
    trade with, 11, 14, 21, 33–34, 44

Factories, 49, 52, 65–66, 73, 87
Fair Housing Act (1968), 128–129
Federal Aid Highway Act, 104
Federal government, 104, 107–108, 109–
    114, 120–121, 123, 126, 128–129

and highways, 93, 104, 120–121, 126
and housing, 107–108, 110–112, 114,
    121, 123, 128–129, 150
party politics, 128, 132
and planning, 110
and suburbs, 107–113, 128
tax policy, 110
and utilities, 107, 109
and welfare reform, 151
Federal Housing Act of 1949, 110–111,
    121
Federal Housing Act of 1954, 110–111,
    121
Federal Housing Administration (FHA),
    107–108, 111–112, 114
    608 Program, 111
    Title VI regulations, 111
Feminism, 119–120, 149
Film, 87, 98, 137
    theaters, 126–127
Finance, 33, 41, 52, 65, 76, 86–87, 93, 95,
    107, 119, 138–139, 145
    of real estate, 41, 76, 87, 95–96, 139,
    145
    of utilities, 107
Fire, 28, 37, 52–53, 59–60, 71, 129
    and building safety, 71
    prevention, 59
Fortifications, 12, 21, 35
France, 10, 16, 21, 26, 49
Franklin, Benjamin, 26, 49
French and Indian War, 26

Gangs, 59–60, 78, 150
Garbage, 13, 22, 35, 127, 131, 151
Gas, 35, 50, 76, 139
    manufacture of, 35, 50
    storage, 50
Gated communities, 145
Gentrification, 140, 143
George, Henry, 73
GI Bill, 114
Gold, 49

Government, 15, 17, 27, 59, 79, 128. *See also* Federal government; Municipal government
Great Lakes, 33
Grocery stores, 126

Higher education, 14, 80, 113–114, 125, 132, 137–139
Highways, 93, 104, 113, 120–121, 126, 145
    and eminent domain, 120
    federal building of, 93, 104, 120–121, 126
    and "freeway revolt," 120
Historic preservation, 140, 142, 146
Homelessness, 121–122, 143
Home Owners' Loan Corporation (HOLC), 107
Hoover, Herbert, 107
Hope VI program, 150
Horsecars, 50, 53, 66, 74
Horses, 35. *See also* Horsecars
Hospitals, 113, 142–143
Hotels, 37, 70, 143
Housing, 22, 24, 34–35, 37, 39, 41, 44, 52–53, 55–56, 65, 79, 87, 90, 93, 107–108, 110–112, 119, 121–123, 128–129, 131, 143–144, 148–150. *See also* Public housing
    abandonment of, 131, 151
    affordability, 143–144, 148
    of African-Americans, 108, 114, 128–129
    colonial types, 22, 24
    in downtown, 140
    of factory workers, 65
    federal role in, 107–113, 114, 119, 121, 123, 128, 150
    nineteenth-century construction, 35, 37, 39
    ownership, 93, 107–108, 119, 140
    of the poor, 53, 55–56, 71, 93, 107–108, 121, 123
    prefabrication of, 112

renting, 34, 41, 44, 55, 93, 108, 123
    segregation, 52, 108, 128–129
    of the wealthy, 50, 53, 56, 79, 87, 90
Huguenots, 16

Illegal drug use, 122, 132
Immigration, 4, 16, 24–25, 39, 43, 49, 58–59, 71, 77, 79, 85–86, 91, 96–97, 113, 150–151
    from Africa, 150
    from China, 71, 77, 150
    from England, 16, 49, 58
    from Europe, 16, 25, 49, 87
    from France, 49
    from Germany, 25, 49, 55, 58–59, 74, 77, 85
    from Greece, 71, 128
    from Holland, 16
    from India, 151
    from Ireland, 49, 55, 58–59, 74, 77, 79, 97, 128
    from Italy, 77, 128
    of Jews, 71, 74, 77, 79, 97
    from Korea, 150
    of Latinos, 150
    Middle Eastern, 71, 150–151
    from Poland, 128
    from Puerto Rico, 113
    of Scotch-Irish, 25
    from Scotland, 49
    segregation and, 39
    into suburbs, 151
    from Vietnam, 150
    from West Indies, 97, 113, 150
Industrialization, 49–50, 65
Insurance, 87, 107, 114
Internet, 153
Iron, 50, 53

Jacobs, Jane, 3
Japan, 14
Jefferson, Thomas, 42, 61
Jews, 15, 25, 71, 74, 77, 79–80, 97, 108, 142

discrimination against, 77, 80, 108
heritage, 142
immigration, 71, 74, 77, 79, 97
Journeymen, 39, 41–42

Kennedy, John F., 114
King Philip's War, 10
Korea, 103, 128, 150
war in, 103, 128

Labor relations, 42, 73–74, 85, 104
and Communism, 104
and law, 42, 73–74
in nineteenth-century City, 42, 73–74
in twentieth-century City, 85, 104
Landfill, 39, 66, 127
Land use, 22, 34, 52, 65, 87. *See also*
Zoning
in colonial City, 22
segregation of, 52
Land values, 4, 34, 58, 96
Law, 42, 73–74, 114, 129
and labor, 42, 73–74
and racial discrimination, 114, 129–130
Le Havre, 14, 33
Lifestyle centers, 145
Lighting, 35, 50, 53
of housing, 50
of streets, 35, 50
Lisbon, 14
Liverpool, 33
London, 3, 14, 21–22, 27, 35, 56, 67
Los Angeles, 2
Lynch, Kevin, 3

Malls, 107, 125, 139–140, 145
Manufacturing, 33, 35, 43, 65, 86–87,
106, 125, 128, 137–138
of computer hardware, 138
decentralization of, 106
decline, 125, 137
of gas, 35, 50
of health care machinery, 138
of textiles, 43, 60

Merchants, 12–15, 21, 25, 27, 33, 37, 44,
58
of colonial City, 12–15, 21, 25, 27
of nineteenth-century City, 33, 37, 44,
58
Mobile homes, 113
Mortgaging, 41, 76, 95–96, 114, 139, 152
subprime mortgage crisis, 152
Movies. *See* Film
Municipal government, 15, 17, 27, 59, 79,
123, 127, 144
of colonial City, 15, 17, 27
of nineteenth-century City, 59, 79
of suburbs, 123, 127, 144
Museums, 80, 139, 143

National Association for the Advancement
of Colored People, 97
National Association of Real Estate Boards,
110
National Conference on Home Building
and Home Ownership, 107
National Interstate and Defense Highways
Act, 120
Native Americans. *See* Amerindians
Nativism, 59–60, 85
New Deal, 104, 108
New Orleans, 33
Newspapers, 27, 69, 79, 86, 111, 137
New urbanism, 142
New York City, 1–2, 11, 14, 34
Nixon, Richard M., 123, 127
Nonprofit agencies, 151
Northwest Ordinance, 34
Nuclear power, 127

Office space, 49, 53, 58, 65, 69–70,
86–87, 89–91, 120–121, 137, 143,
145
in downtown, 53, 65, 69–70, 86–87,
89–91, 121, 137, 143
in suburbs, 120–121, 145
Oil, 120, 131, 139
Organization of Petroleum Exporting
Countries (OPEC), 120

Paine, Thomas, 42
Parking, 110, 121–122, 126, 139
Parks, 35, 66, 95, 122
Parkways, 104
Pedestrians, 50, 66, 142
Penn, William, 10, 34
Peru, 14
Philadelphia, 1–2, 12, 34
Philanthropy. *See* Charity
Pigs, 22, 35, 55
Planned unit development, 139, 148
Playgrounds, 95
Pollution, 52, 127, 142, 146
Popular culture, 97
Population decline, 119, 130
Population growth, 33, 49, 65, 71, 85,
    104, 106, 119, 137, 153
  in suburbs, 85, 104, 106, 119, 137
Port Authority, 139
Port facilities, 22, 38, 85, 103, 122, 127,
    139–140, 142
  of colonial City, 22
  naval use of, 103, 142
  of nineteenth-century City, 38
  renewal, 122, 140, 142
  of twentieth-century city, 85, 103, 122,
    127, 139
Poverty, 28, 35, 43, 53, 55–56, 59, 71, 93,
    108, 121, 144
  in colonial City, 28
  in nineteenth-century City, 35, 43, 53,
    55–56, 59, 71
  in suburbs, 144
  in twentieth-century City, 93, 108, 121
Privateering, 26
Prostitution, 44, 78, 122
Protestantism, 11, 17, 59–60, 77–78, 80,
    128
Public education, 42, 77, 129–130, 138,
    144
Public health, 14, 21, 25, 27, 52, 55–56,
    71–72, 91, 125, 127, 142, 151
  in colonial City, 14, 21, 25, 27

in nineteenth-century City, 52, 55–56,
  71–72
and pollution, 127
research in, 125
sanitary regulation, 55–56, 71, 91
in twentieth-century City, 91, 125, 127,
  142–143
Public housing, 108, 122, 150
  architecture of, 122
Public markets, 22, 35
Public-private partnerships, 122, 126, 143,
  151
Public transportation, 50, 56, 145, 149
Publishing, 98, 107
Pullman Porters Union, 113
Puritans, 13–14, 25

Quakers, 14–15
Quebec, 21

Radio, 86–87, 98
Railroads, 4, 49–50, 52–53, 65–67, 69, 87,
  97, 112, 121, 126–127, 139, 144
Randolph, A. Philip, 113
Real estate development, 34, 41, 56,
  75–76, 87–89, 91, 93–95, 107–108,
  110, 140, 145
  downtown, 88–89, 140
  employment in, 107
  finance of, 41, 76, 87, 95, 145
  and housing interests, 108
  public-private partnerships, 122
  and streetcars, 75–76
  suburban, 75–76, 94, 112–113
Recession. *See* Economic recession
Redlining, 108, 128–129
Red Scare, 104
Refrigerators, 86, 127
Republican party, 128
Restaurants, 37, 70, 140
Restrictive covenants, 76–77, 91, 145
Retail, 22, 37, 49, 53, 56, 58, 65, 69–70,
  75, 86–87, 93, 96, 107, 112, 125–126,
  140, 142–143, 145

in colonial City, 22
concentration of, 53, 56
downtown, 53, 56, 65, 69–70, 86–87,
107, 142–143
in nineteenth-century City, 37, 49, 53,
58
strip forms, 75, 93, 112, 125–126
suburbanization of, 107, 123, 125, 145
Riots, 27, 59–60, 97, 113, 130
race-related, 97, 113, 130

St. Louis, 33
Sanitation. *See* Public health
Scientific invention, 49, 55
Scientific revolution, 14
Scotch-Irish, 25
Section 8 grants, 123
Sewers, 50, 52, 76, 107, 109, 148
federal subsidy of, 107, 109
Shelly v. Kramer, 114
Shipbuilding, 37, 50
Sidewalks, 34–35, 95, 142
Skyscrapers, 66, 69, 87, 89–90
Slavery, 11, 13, 15, 24–25, 28–29, 33, 44,
59
abolition, 44, 59
and West Indies, 25, 28–29
Slums, 50, 52–54, 71, 108, 111, 121
clearance of, 111, 121
Smart growth, 149
Socialism, 59, 74, 85
Soviet Union, 103
Spain, 14, 16
Stagflation, 119
Steam ferries, 33, 50
Streetcars, 4, 66–67, 69, 74–76, 87, 93,
121, 127, 150
and real estate development, 75–76
and suburbanization, 75–76, 87
Streets, 13, 22, 50, 66, 69, 76, 94
of colonial City, 13, 22
gridding, 34
lighting, 35, 50
paving, 34, 66

in suburbs, 94
and utilities, 76
Strikes, 42, 60, 73, 79, 103
Subdivision, 12, 22, 34–35, 69, 76, 93–95,
139
in colonial City, 12, 22
of planned unit developments, 139
and suburbanization, 76, 94–95, 139
Suburbs, 4, 33, 56, 75, 85–87, 93–96,
104, 106–108, 109–113, 119–120,
123, 125–128, 130–131, 137, 139,
144–149, 151–152
architecture, 56, 94, 111, 125
diversity in, 151
employment, 123, 125, 145
environmentalism, 127, 146
federal role in development of, 107–113,
119
government of, 123
industry, 111, 125
lifestyles, 131
population, 85, 104, 106, 119, 137
poverty, 144
real estate development, 75–76, 94,
112–113
redlining, 108, 128–129
retail, 107, 123, 125–126, 145
and steam ferries, 33
and streetcars, 75, 87
streets, 94
subdivision, 76, 93–95
and subprime mortgage crisis, 152
taxes, 125–127, 144, 149
utilities, 95, 109
Subways, 67, 87, 89, 121
Sustainability, 146
*Swann v. Charlotte-Mecklenburg Board of
Education*, 129
Synagogues, 22, 97

Taxes, 27, 73, 110, 125, 144, 149, 151
in colonial City, 27
federal deductions of, 110
foreclosure and, 151

in nineteenth-century City, 73
in suburbs, 125–127, 144, 149
in twentieth-century City, 131
Telegraph, 49, 52, 67, 69, 90
Telephones, 69, 87, 90, 131
Television, 131, 137
Tenements, 55, 71, 93, 107
Textile mills, 43
Theaters, 70, 87, 126
Tocqueville, Alexis de, 61
Trade, 9–12, 14, 21, 25–26, 33–34, 44, 50, 52, 60, 85, 139
  by air, 139
  with American interior, 33
  with American South, 60
  among Amerindians, 9
  with Asia, 11, 14, 33
  with Europe, 11, 14, 21, 33–34, 44
  of slaves, 11, 25
  with West Indies, 21, 26
Tradesmen, 39, 41–42, 58, 74
Traffic congestion, 66–67, 93, 110, 145
Trucking, 126
Truman, Harry S., 103, 113
Turnpikes, 33, 144

Unions, 42, 59, 73–74, 79, 85, 103–104, 113, 137
U.S. Bureau of Roads, 104
U.S. Routes, 93, 104, 106, 112, 145
Urban Land Institute, 110
Urban renewal, 110–111, 113, 121–123, 139
  architecture of, 122–123
  of downtown, 122–123, 139
  of port facilities, 122, 139
Utilities, 50, 52–53, 76, 95, 107
  federal subsidy, 107
  in suburbs, 95, 107

Vietnam, 103, 119–120, 128, 131, 150
  immigration from, 150
  war in, 103, 119–120, 128, 131
Visa, 114

Wages, 55, 151
Wagner-Steagall Act, 108
Warehousing, 37, 50, 52, 65–66, 87, 122, 126
Waterfront. See Port facilities
Water supply, 52, 71, 76, 107, 109, 127
  federal role in, 107, 109, 127
Welfare reform, 151
West Indies, 14, 21, 25–26, 28, 97, 113, 150
  immigration from, 97, 113, 150
  and slavery, 25, 28
  trade with, 26
Wharves. See Port facilities
White flight, 128, 130–131
Witchcraft, 28
Women, 28, 42, 44, 49, 59, 119, 132
  in colonial City, 28
  domestic life, 28, 44, 149
  employment, 42, 132, 149
  and feminism, 119–120, 149
  in nineteenth-century City, 42
  and prostitution, 44
  rights, 59, 119–120
Working classes, 39, 67, 71, 79, 121, 128, 132, 138–140, 150
  employment, 71, 132, 139
  neighborhoods, 67, 121, 128, 140, 150
World War I, 86, 126
World War II, 104, 106, 110, 113, 122, 127, 142

Zoning, 52, 66, 76, 87, 91, 111, 140, 144, 148–149

Maureen Smith, *The U.S. Paper Industry and Sustainable Production: An Argument for Restructuring*

Keith Pezzoli, *Human Settlements and Planning for Ecological Sustainability: The Case of Mexico City*

Sarah Hammond Creighton, *Greening the Ivory Tower: Improving the Environmental Track Record of Universities, Colleges, and Other Institutions*

Jan Mazurek, *Making Microchips: Policy, Globalization, and Economic Restructuring in the Semiconductor Industry*

William A. Shutkin, *The Land That Could Be: Environmentalism and Democracy in the Twenty-First Century*

Richard Hofrichter, ed., *Reclaiming the Environmental Debate: The Politics of Health in a Toxic Culture*

Robert Gottlieb, *Environmentalism Unbound: Exploring New Pathways for Change*

Kenneth Geiser, *Materials Matter: Toward a Sustainable Materials Policy*

Thomas D. Beamish, *Silent Spill: The Organization of an Industrial Crisis*

Matthew Gandy, *Concrete and Clay: Reworking Nature in New York City*

David Naguib Pellow, *Garbage Wars: The Struggle for Environmental Justice in Chicago*

Julian Agyeman, Robert D. Bullard, and Bob Evans, eds., *Just Sustainabilities: Development in an Unequal World*

Barbara L. Allen, *Uneasy Alchemy: Citizens and Experts in Louisiana's Chemical Corridor Disputes*

Dara O'Rourke, *Community-Driven Regulation: Balancing Development and the Environment in Vietnam*

Brian K. Obach, *Labor and the Environmental Movement: The Quest for Common Ground*

Peggy F. Barlett and Geoffrey W. Chase, eds., *Sustainability on Campus: Stories and Strategies for Change*

Steve Lerner, *Diamond: A Struggle for Environmental Justice in Louisiana's Chemical Corridor*

Jason Corburn, *Street Science: Community Knowledge and Environmental Health Justice*

Peggy F. Barlett, ed., *Urban Place: Reconnecting with the Natural World*

David Naguib Pellow and Robert J. Brulle, eds., *Power, Justice, and the Environment: A Critical Appraisal of the Environmental Justice Movement*

Eran Ben-Joseph, *The Code of the City: Standards and the Hidden Language of Place Making*

Nancy J. Myers and Carolyn Raffensperger, eds., *Precautionary Tools for Reshaping Environmental Policy*

Kelly Sims Gallagher, *China Shifts Gears: Automakers, Oil, Pollution, and Development*

Kerry H. Whiteside, *Precautionary Politics: Principle and Practice in Confronting Environmental Risk*

Ronald Sandler and Phaedra C. Pezzullo, eds., *Environmental Justice and Environmentalism: The Social Justice Challenge to the Environmental Movement*

Julie Sze, *Noxious New York: The Racial Politics of Urban Health and Environmental Justice*

Robert D. Bullard, ed., *Growing Smarter: Achieving Livable Communities, Environmental Justice, and Regional Equity*

Ann Rappaport and Sarah Hammond Creighton, *Degrees That Matter: Climate Change and the University*

Michael Egan, *Barry Commoner and the Science of Survival: The Remaking of American Environmentalism*

David J. Hess, *Alternative Pathways in Science and Industry: Activism, Innovation, and the Environment in an Era of Globalization*

Peter F. Cannavò, *The Working Landscape: Founding, Preservation, and the Politics of Place*

Paul Stanton Kibel, ed., *Rivertown: Rethinking Urban Rivers*

Kevin P. Gallagher and Lyuba Zarsky, *The Enclave Economy: Foreign Investment and Sustainable Development in Mexico's Silicon Valley*

David Naguib Pellow, *Resisting Global Toxics: Transnational Movements for Environmental Justice*

Robert Gottlieb, *Reinventing Los Angeles: Nature and Community in the Global City*

David V. Carruthers, ed., *Environmental Justice in Latin America: Problems, Promise, and Practice*

Tom Angotti, *New York for Sale: Community Planning Confronts Global Real Estate*

Paloma Pavel, ed., *Breakthrough Communities: Sustainability and Justice in the Next American Metropolis*

Anastasia Loukaitou-Sideris and Renia Ehrenfeucht, *Sidewalks: Conflict and Negotiation over Public Space*

David J. Hess, *Localist Movements in a Global Economy: Sustainability, Justice, and Urban Development in the United States*

Julian Agyeman and Yelena Ogneva-Himmelberger, eds., *Environmental Justice and Sustainability in the Former Soviet Union*

Jason Corburn, *Toward the Healthy City: People, Places, and the Politics of Urban Planning*

JoAnn Carmin and Julian Agyeman, eds., *Environmental Inequalities beyond Borders: Local Perspectives on Global Injustices*

Louise Mozingo, *Pastoral Capitalism: A History of Suburban Corporate Landscapes*

Gwen Ottinger and Benjamin Cohen, eds., *Technoscience and Environmental Justice: Expert Cultures in a Grassroots Movement*

Samantha MacBride, *Recycling Reconsidered: The Present Failure and Future Promise of Environmental Action in the United States*

Andrew Karvonen, *Politics of Urban Runoff: Nature, Technology, and the Sustainable City*

Daniel Schneider, *Hybrid Nature: Sewage Treatment and the Creation of the Industrial Ecosystem*

Catherine Tumber, *Small, Gritty, and Green: The Promise of America's Smaller Industrial Cities in a Low-Carbon World*

Sam Bass Warner and Andrew H. Whittemore, *American Urban Form: A Representative History*

Printed in the United States
by Baker & Taylor Publisher Services